THE
WIND
AND THE
RUDDER

THE
WIND
AND THE
RUDDER

How to Live in the Power of the Spirit
Without Becoming Weird

DAN SMITH

DESTINY IMAGE₍ᵣ₎ PUBLISHERS, INC.
P.O. Box 310, Shippensburg, PA 17257-0310
"Promoting Inspired Lives."

This book and all other Destiny Image, Revival Press, MercyPlace, Fresh Bread, Destiny Image Fiction, and Treasure House books are available at Christian bookstores and distributors worldwide.

For a U.S. bookstore nearest you, call 1-800-722-6774.
For more information on foreign distributors, call 717-532-3040.
Reach us on the Internet: www.destinyimage.com.

ISBN 13 TP: 978-0-7684-0284-1
ISBN 13 Ebook: 978-0-7684-8805-0

For Worldwide Distribution, Printed in the U.S.A.
1 2 3 4 5 6 7 8 / 16 15 14 13 12

ACKNOWLEDGMENTS

This book is the fruit of God working through many people in my life. They have contributed greatly, both personally and professionally, and I am eternally grateful to each of them. I would like to recognize them here.

My wife, Jane, has provided a safe and peaceful place to live and work. Her love and encouragement gave me a solid foundation and helped me to see this project through to the end. She was an enormous help to me as my first editor. I love you, Jane!

My daughters, Stephanie and Lindsey, along with Lindsey's husband, Brent, are some of my biggest fans, and their love and encouragement has been a tremendous help and source of strength.

My associate and friend, Mike Flynn, who has authored five books himself, was a great help in editing the manuscript, and in providing practical suggestions along the way. Mike, I hope to keep learning from you and look forward to enjoying more times together at Starbucks.

My friend, Dr. Marèque Ireland, invested much of her time in reading portions of the manuscript and made many helpful suggestions, especially with Chapter 2. Her comments and corrections as a theologian have enabled me to represent the Holy Spirit more accurately, and have made this a better book.

To the wonderful people of the Vineyard Community Church in Camarillo: You are simply the best people any pastor could hope for, and I couldn't have done any of this without your love, prayers, and encouragement.

I especially want to thank Bert Waggoner, who, although he carries the enormous weight of leading the Vineyard movement, took the time to read the entire manuscript, and to offer valuable insights and analysis. I can think of no one I would rather have written the forward to this book. Thank you Bert!

I also need to express my heartfelt thanks to Vinson Synan, Todd Hunter, Jeremy Begbie, Jason Bridge, Phil Guthrie, Ray Batt, Aaron Dunn, Roy Bach, Rick Wright, Rick Taylor, and Patrick Baligasima. They all read the manuscript and gave me both great encouragement and helpful suggestions.

Special thanks to Doug Addison, who not only read the manuscript, but introduced me to Drew Rivera at Destiny Image. Your ministry continues to bring joy and freedom to many!

Thank you, Mom and Dad, for laying such a firm foundation of faith in Jesus. You introduced me to the Wind and provided the rudder for my life. And thanks, Mom Williams, who was such a prayer warrior and source of inspiration.

I will always owe a debt of gratitude to John Wimber, the founder of the Vineyard movement. Thanks, John, for modeling humility and love for the whole Church. You taught me so much and impacted my life profoundly. And thanks for the costly price you paid to give birth to and lead this movement.

Finally, I want to thank Drew Rivera and the team at Destiny Image for believing in me as a first-time author, and for working with me to make this dream become reality.

ENDORSEMENTS

The Wind and the Rudder is an inspirational and instructive work on "how to live joyfully in the power of the Holy Spirit." Dan Smith is not an armchair theoretician; he has experienced and practiced the life in the Spirit he writes about. I encourage all who are thirsty to experience more of God to make *The Wind and the Rudder* a priority read.

BERTEN WAGGONER
National Director
Vineyard USA

This is a very well-written and timely book. I recommend it to anyone who longs to know and experience more of the Holy Spirit.

VINSON SYNAN
Dean Emeritus
Regent University
School of Divinity (Virginia Beach)

The Wind and the Rudder gives you great biblical foundation for living a life directed by the Holy Spirit. Dan Smith has a way of making things naturally supernatural. This book is full of foundational teaching, practical stories, and examples from history. Your life will never be the same!

DOUG ADDISON
Author of *Personal Development God's Way*
www.dougaddison.com

The New Testament envisions a conversational relationship with the Holy Spirit that builds up the Church and provides gifts and power to serve the world. But many of us have a difficult time finding such a relationship. It seems too hard to navigate waters that easily become weird. And it surely can invite controversy. But we have no choice. There can be no Christianity without the Holy Spirit front and center. If you are being led to explore the person and work of the Holy Spirit, Dan Smith, while you may not agree with every word he writes, is a veteran and reliable guide.

TODD HUNTER
Anglican Bishop
Past President, Vineyard Churches USA
Past President, Alpha USA
Author of *Our Favorite Sins* (Thomas Nelson Publishers, 2012)

Dan is a spiritual father many of us would like be associated with, and I highly recommend all believers and ministers alike to read this book.

APOSTLE PATRICK BALIGASIMA
Founder/President
Discipleship Missions Int. (Uganda)

The Lord is about to pour out His Spirit in new and amazing ways. Most Christians are excited about this, but are unaware that God wants to use them. Dan's book, *The Wind and the Rudder*, will not only open your eyes to see what God has already begun to do in our generation, but it will cause you to hunger for all that He has for you. It will teach you how to be prepared and equipped so you can step into your destiny, so your life can make a difference on earth for such a time as this.

RICK TAYLOR
Director of the Healing Rooms
of the Santa Maria Valley

If the Spirit-led life has baffled you at times, this book is the key to unlock those mysteries. In my 20 years of ministry I have yet to run across a writing that so brilliantly explains the complexities of what it means to work in partnership with the Holy Spirit like *The Wind and the Rudder* does. Dan Smith has penned a book for ministers and lay people that will enhance your walk with the Lord and give the biblical balance that is so needed in the lives of the 21st-century Christ-follower. Pick it up today, read it tomorrow, and begin putting it into practice the next day.

AARON DUNN
Pastor of Assimilation and Volunteer Ministries
Phoenix First Assembly
Phoenix, Arizona

Dan Smith's book is a welcome and timely contribution to the Church. His passion for God and heart for people shine through each page as he shares with us his insight on the person and work of the Holy Spirit. Stemming from a lifetime of ministry, deep prayer, biblical study, and personal experience, Smith inspires us to embrace our identity as persons empowered and led by the Spirit. This book is not only for those who wish to be better equipped for ministry, but for anyone who wishes to deepen their sensitivity to and understanding of God's personal and active presence in the person of the Spirit.

MARÈQUE STEELE IRELAND
Affiliate Assistant Professor of Theology
Fuller Theological Seminary

If there is ever a time for a powerful book like this, that time is *now!* *The Wind and the Rudder* is an amazing reminder that, as we "do life," there is a wonderful helper who empowers us to fulfill our promised destiny—a destiny we were not created to fulfill alone. So sit back, and allow God, through His Spirit, to fill your sail with an undeniable power, which will revive you and bring joy back into the journey.

JASON BRIDGE
Senior Pastor, Word of Life Family Church
Phillips, Wisconsin

The Greek word translated "disciple" (*mathetes*) literally means "learner." Dan Smith is a long-term learner. This book is not theoretical; it comes out of practical experience in putting the Word of God to work. I have worked with Dan for 9 years and have found him to be a practitioner of the things he writes about in this book. The word "balance" well describes him: he goes all out for the things God puts on his heart and he doesn't permit success to influence his ability to assess things maturely. You will enjoy the forthright stories in this book as well as the conclusions Dan draws out of them. If you put them into practice you'll find that this book has changed your life.

REV. MIKE FLYNN
Founder and Director of FreshWind Ministries

A warm and passionate testimony to the creative, renewing energy of the Holy Spirit, drawing on years of pastoral experience. At a time when the Church desperately needs to "sail with the wind," there is much here to ponder and take to heart.

JEREMY BEGBIE
Duke University

I enthusiastically recommend *The Wind and the Rudder*. For those of us with eyes to see, we will receive a picture of what the Spirit of Jesus is preparing for His beloved Bride. Biblical and historical examples of the work of His Spirit are woven throughout the pages. The author is a seeker; a man of integrity whom I have known for 25 years. Maturity and spiritual sensitivity will be needed for the glorious days ahead. Like a compass, *The Wind and the Rudder* points us to the coming King.

PHIL GUTHRIE
Founder and President, Radio Nueva Vida

Scripture says there is a river that makes glad the people of God. That river is the Holy Spirit. The early Church learned to work with the Spirit, and that made all the difference. Dan gives us clear instructions, personal experience, and wonderful stories that will help us navigate the river of God in the coming harvest revival. Dan's book, if believed, will help us not miss our day of visitation.

RICK WRIGHT
Senior Pastor, The Gathering Place
Studio City, California

CONTENTS

FOREWORD

THERE WAS A TIME, AND it was not long ago, that the Evangelical church and much of the rest of the church was afraid of the gifts of the Spirit. Praying for the sick, speaking in tongues, and prophesying were at the least held suspect or at the most demonic. Theologies had developed that said all of these gifts and many more had been a vital part of New Testament experience, but with the full development of the Bible, they were no longer needed and thus ceased to operate when the canon was closed. The Bible then replaced the Spirit; it became the only way that God could speak.

But things have changed. Early in the twentieth century the Pentecostal movement erupted on the world scene that caused a tsunami of the Spirit accompanied with signs following such as those once rejected or ignored gifts. This was followed in the Sixties by a second spiritual tsunami called the Charismatic movement that upset the spiritual landscape in old-line denominations, the Roman Catholic church, and many Evangelical churches. Though many in the church would continue to say that they are neither Charismatic nor Pentecostal, they would also go on to say that they believe all of the gifts of the Spirit are for today and that they want those gifts to be expressed in their churches. It could be rightly said that the twentieth century was a century in which the Holy Spirit's work was forcefully felt through all the church.

An ever-increasing number of books are being written on the Holy Spirit by scholars and practitioners across the theological spectrum. Yet they are not only writing about the Holy Spirit in redemption—inspiring the Bible, convicting sinners, illuminating the Word. These are all very important functions of the Spirit, but they are only a small part of the Spirit's work. There is much more. The Spirit speaks to us, gifts us to serve both in the church and the world, and anoints us to do the works of Jesus such as preaching the gospel, healing the sick, and freeing people from spiritual bondage. The Spirit builds the church to be a reconciling community that breaks down the walls of prejudice, destroys sectarianism, and cares for creation. There is nothing in our lives that the Spirit is not related to in some way.

The Wind and the Rudder adds another very helpful book to this genre. It is a very practical guide for those who want to live in the Spirit and who need some skills to help them do so. It is not written by an armchair theoretician. Dan is an experienced practitioner who has learned to live naturally in the supernatural. He has prayed for the sick, prophesied, and cast out demons. He not only tells you what the Spirit wants to do in your life, he also shows from years of experience how to cooperate with the Spirit in a non-religious way. Your heart will be warmed, your mind will be challenged, and your faith will be strengthened in the reading.

BERTEN A. WAGGONER
National Director
Vineyard USA

INTRODUCTION

THE NEXT GREAT AWAKENING HAS already begun.

In Santa Maria, California, the Healing Rooms, staffed by volunteers from over 30 local churches, have seen hundreds of medically verified healings of every imaginable disease, and are seeing people come to Christ almost daily.

An evangelist with InterVarsity in Los Angeles told me that he recently gave an altar call at a secular university and was stunned when over 50 students responded to the invitation to receive Christ. When I asked him if this was becoming a trend, he said, "Definitely."

A group of Christians, trained in "prophetic evangelism," recently staffed a booth at the Santa Barbara County Fair, on which they put a sign, "Refreshment for the Journey." They engaged curious individuals in conversation, giving them words of prophetic encouragement and insight (what many would call "Words of Knowledge"). Such was their impact that they were awarded First Prize in the non-profit category!

In Redding, California, an army of youth regularly invade local malls, praying for strangers that they had earlier received clues about in prayer circles, often with dramatic results (they call these outreaches "Treasure Hunts"). Their church has become a training ground for young people from all over the country who are desperate for the power of the Spirit.

Radio Nueva Vida, based in Camarillo, California, has become the largest Spanish Christian radio network in America. My friend, Phil Guthrie, who is the president and founder, shares with me week after week amazing stories of hundreds upon hundreds of people finding Christ through their broadcasts. They regularly see people healed and delivered from demons right in their offices. God is bringing revival to the Spanish-speaking population in the U.S.!

This is only a small sampling of evidence that I have seen in the last year or so, but I would bet many of you can testify to similar things, and even greater works of the Spirit in your own communities. Thousands of people across the U.S. have been praying for a nationwide revival, and I just don't believe that God will ignore their cries. Someone has said, "Whenever God is ready to do something big, He sets His people praying." We have all heard stories of how the Spirit has been moving with power in other countries, and many of us are getting tired of being long-distance spectators. You may even be burned out as you read this book, but be encouraged—God has not forgotten you, and God has not forgotten America.

In my own church, we have been sensing a growing desperation for a massive outpouring of God's Spirit, and as I have interacted with other pastors, I'm finding the same thing happening in other churches across the country. The Holy Spirit is up to something big and we need to prepare.

The outpouring of God's Spirit is the primary thing, but not the only thing we need. There have been many times in history when the wind of God's Spirit has begun to move powerfully through an individual, in a city or across a nation, only to see healthy, long-lasting revival aborted due to the lack of a rudder. One of the attempts of this book is to help provide the stabilizing force of a strong rudder during times of dramatic renewal and revival.

Adventure............... Mystery............... Power............... Grace............ Satisfaction............... Destiny............... Favor.

These are a few of the things we are meant to experience when participating with Jesus in this incredible mission He has called us to. When He lived among us, the Spirit led Him into one adventure after another. He was anything but predictable, conventional, or conforming. He was adored by outcasts, hated by the establishment, and followed by thousands. The message He preached was revolutionary, challenging, and compelling. Those who were privileged to know Him intimately were changed forever. They had been caught in His gravitational pull, and were undone, or broken, or awestruck. But they all knew, in a way they had never known before, how deeply they were loved, how much they would suffer, and how great was their destiny. They would become world-changers.

"The Blackbird" is the nickname for the SR-71, perhaps the most highly developed strategic reconnaissance plane ever built. It was designed with a metal skin that would expand because of the heat from of flying so high and so fast. It was built with six expansion points, enabling it to literally stretch in flight. It was truly a miracle of engineering. However, when it was sitting on the ground, it would leak fuel all over the place from those relaxed expansion points, needing drip pans placed under it, like an old car in a stained driveway, and was anything but impressive.

All of this was by design, and it is a picture of the Christian. We have been designed for supersonic flight and mind-numbing performance. We have been designed to be like Jesus. He modeled the Spirit-empowered life, challenged His disciples to do the impossible (like feed thousands with a boy's lunch, or walk on water, or cast out stubborn demons), and seemed frustrated when they couldn't. There is a whole dimension of living that has gone un-experienced by most followers of Jesus, and He still waits. We are like the Blackbird, designed for greatness and lofty flight, but, sadly, most of the time we sit in the hangar, unimpressive. We sit earth-bound.

There are also a few Blackbirds who fly fast and high, but, like the early prototypes, have flaws that make them unstable, and sometimes the consequences are disastrous. The faster we fly, the more crucial the stabilizing systems become. At the risk of mixing metaphors, we are like sailing ships, designed for Wind power and helpless without it, but once the Wind begins to blow and the sails are raised, the integrity of the rudder becomes most important.

A "revelation," for lack of a better word, came to me about 17 years ago, during a prayer meeting in Canada, and was accompanied by a mental picture. In this picture, I saw an old ship, perhaps something out of the 17th or 18th century. The ship had masts, but the sails were tied up and had not been used for some time because the sea was dead calm, and there had been no wind for a long time. As a result, the sailors were struggling hard with many oars, similar to the old Viking ships, with rows of sailors on each side, rowing hard to propel the heavy vessel.

Then something interesting happened: The wind began to blow, and as the wind blew, the sailors looked around, a little confused, because it had been so long since they had sailed with the wind behind them, and for a while they didn't know how to respond. At first a few, then others, began heading for the sails, to unfurl them. One by one the sails began to fill with the wind, and the sailors started pulling in the oars. As the ship picked up speed, the sails now completely deployed and filled with wind, the sailors began smiling, looking at one another, some even laughing, as fatigue gave way to joy and relief.

One of the reasons for writing this book is to share what God has taught me since that "revelation" 17 years ago, as I have sought Him for clarity and understanding, and as I have attempted to put those things into practice in my own church. If we believe that there is another historic windstorm of God's Spirit about to be poured out across the earth, then it is time to learn a new set of skills because what many of us have been prepared for is "rowing," but for what is coming we will need to learn to sail!

The Body of Christ, and particularly those in leadership, has largely become accustomed to a mode of ministry that is laborious and exhausting. But there are strong indications that there is a new and wonderful season dawning upon us, bringing a momentum of the Spirit that will radically change the way many of us experience church.

I've been a Christian most of my life (except for a four-year period of rebellion, between the ages of 17 and 21). As a pastor's kid, I saw my parents put in many long hours of hard work, and suffer much heartache, while doing the "work of the ministry." And having been a pastor myself for over 30 years, my wife and I know what it is to labor, plan, strategize, recruit, motivate, teach, and suffer disappointment. I understand the self-doubt, the battles against all forms of temptation, the constant struggle not to compare myself with other, more "successful" pastors, the yearning for a richer harvest and healthier disciples, the occasional burnout, the sickness of heart over hope deferred, and countless other challenges faced daily by thousands of pastors and leaders. I have also experienced those welcome surges of Spirit-given momentum that bring new hope, joy, relief, and power, like the wind filling the sails of the old ship, and I am one voice in a growing chorus that is shouting, "The Wind is coming again!"

This book is written, both for those who identify themselves as Evangelicals and for those who call themselves

Pentecostals/Charismatics (although, many of us are, in fact, a mixture), and for the many Catholics and members of mainline denominations who truly love Jesus. It is written out of a great love for the whole Body of Christ, and with a passion that all of us become skilled at learning to minister effectively and powerfully in the footsteps of Jesus. For many of us, this means learning a new appreciation for and understanding of what it means to work in partnership with the Holy Spirit and making the necessary adjustments, so that we can move forward with Kingdom effectiveness and theological integrity.

But the burden of this book is really two-fold: To help an ocean of Jesus-followers discover the thrill, the adventure, and the passion of the Spirit-filled life they have been called to, and to help other believers, who have had some experience of the Spirit, to discover balance, understanding, and a new sense of mission. We must have both the Wind and the rudder. It is my hope and prayer that this book will help to bring a fresh passion and understanding to the Church of Jesus Christ, and that it may be a helpful tool in the hands of the Spirit to equip and mobilize the army of God for the coming harvest.

Chapter 1

SAILING IS BETTER THAN ROWING

"Since we live by the Spirit, let us keep in step with the Spirit." Galatians 5:25

IT WAS ONE OF THOSE tension-filled days in our home. You've had them, I'm sure. It seemed like everything I said came out wrong, and what was worse was that everything my wife, Jane, or my daughters, Lindsey or Stephanie, said also seemed to come out wrong, or be taken wrong. If our home were a big piece of machinery, it would have sounded horribly noisy, like metal scraping against metal, desperately in need of oil or grease. It was as if everyone had gotten up on the wrong side of bed, and the whole day had gone like that. Finally, some time in the early afternoon, I had to go to the store for something, and, to be honest, was relieved to get out of the house and to enjoy, for a little while, the peace of being by myself in the car.

When I returned and pulled into the driveway, I paused before I turned off the motor and prayed a simple prayer: "Lord, help us. Help us change the atmosphere in our home." Even before I'd finished that short prayer, the words "ice cream" popped into my mind. It all took about five seconds. I went inside and announced to the family, "Let's get out of here and go get some ice cream." Immediately everyone was on the same page—no disagreement here! Within five minutes we were in the car and on our way to the ice cream store, and just like that, the entire mood of our family had changed! We had been rowing; now we were sailing.

There are two distinctly different paradigms for ministry in the church of Jesus Christ. The first paradigm, with which we are all too familiar, is characterized by hard work, long hours of planning, digging for ideas, running to the latest workshops or seminars that promise great results, and often pressuring people to serve in ways that help fulfill someone's vision. This is rowing, and is common in an environment where there is little "wind" of the Spirit.

The second paradigm for ministry also involves planning and effort, to be sure, but of a different kind. This mode of operation takes seriously the partnership dynamic of people working in conjunction with the Holy Spirit. It is more heavily weighted toward prayer, sometimes with fasting, and consciously learning to become sensitive to the impressions given by God—more generously than many realize. This is sailing, and is more common where there is some movement of the Holy Spirit.

A friend of mine, Tom, is a Senior Vice President of Information Systems for a national corporation. He and his staff had been struggling for days to find a solution to a software problem that had all but paralyzed their department. Then one day, as Tom was driving in his car thinking about what to do, it occurred to him that he really hadn't prayed about the situation. So right there, in his car, he asked God to show him what to do. By the time he got back to work, everything started clicking. Suddenly new ideas started coming, creative energy began flowing, and the problem was solved within hours. First they had tried rowing; then came sailing. Sailing is better than rowing!

THE SPIRIT AND MOMENTUM

John Maxwell says momentum makes everything go better and makes everyone look better. Sports teams know this, which is why, when a basketball team begins to rack up points, the opposing coach will often call a time-out. He understands the importance of interrupting the momentum of the other team. When you have momentum going for you, everything seems easier, progress happens more quickly, people are more supportive, your weaknesses are overlooked, your strengths are magnified, and favor seems to come naturally. No wonder Maxwell calls momentum "The Big Mo!" Political campaigns know this, which is why they spend so much time, energy, and money trying to develop it. At a certain point, a wave of energy seems to build, people are more and more inclined to get on board, and it becomes almost impossible to stop.

Before the Day of Pentecost, the disciples were simply waiting. They knew Jesus was alive because He had revealed Himself to them several times since His resurrection. But they didn't know much of anything else. Where do we go from here? What do we do now? So, in obedience to Jesus' instructions, they simply stayed in the city, waiting and praying. Then it happened: Boom! It is significant that the Spirit came *"like a violent rushing wind"* (Acts 2:2 NASB). What better picture of momentum and power could the Spirit Himself have given Luke as he inspired him to write this account in Acts. Momentum is what the Spirit produced on that memorable morning, as that divine wind carried the disciples for years throughout the known world, expanding the kingdom with explosive force and changing history forever.

Patrick Baligasima received Jesus while he was practicing his engineering profession in Uganda, and knew God had called him into full-time pastoral ministry. His father was vehemently opposed, knowing he would have a hard time supporting a family as a pastor, and began telling everyone in his village that his son Patrick had lost his mind. So for a full year, the entire church consisted of Patrick, his wife, and one friend.

Then his father became critically ill and was unable to find a cure, either from doctors or witch doctors. Finally, in desperation, he decided to visit his son. He had decided that if his son's prayer could heal him, he would turn to God. As Patrick began to pray for his father, a demon manifested, and Patrick cast it out. His father was immediately healed, and began testifying all over the village. The following Sunday, 300 people showed up at Patrick's church. From 3 to 300 in one week—that's momentum!

That church has now grown to over 2,500 people, and 400 churches have been planted all over Uganda from that one church. The Spirit of God, through the healing of one man, initiated a wave of momentum that is still sweeping thousands of people into the kingdom. Sailing is better than rowing!

Life is hard. Marriage takes work. Raising kids is a challenge. Ministry of any kind can be a grind, because ministry is just another word for serving, and serving always requires something from you. So whether you're "ministering" to your family or serving at work, or at church, or in your community, you are at risk of being worn down. Statistics indicate that only 10% of pastors are still in the ministry by the age of 65. It simply could not be God's plan that we should be miserable and worn out as a result of serving Him or serving people.

Yes, ministry does require an expenditure of energy. The saying, "no pain, no gain," is accurate, yet there is a "good tired" and a "bad tired." In Ezekiel 44, when God was giving the prophet instructions about the new temple and priesthood, He made it clear that the priests were not to wear woolen garments, but clothes made only of linen, so that they would not perspire. It has been said that some ministers try to compensate by perspiration what they lack in inspiration. This reflects the difference between a paradigm of ministry that is highly dependent on human effort, and a paradigm of ministry that is highly dependent on the power of the Spirit.

When Zerubbabel was frustrated in his efforts to rebuild the temple, God spoke through the prophet Zechariah, "…'Not by might nor by power, but by My Spirit,' says the Lord Almighty…'This mountain (of opposition) shall be removed'" (Zech. 4:6-7 paraphrased). And as we know, in spite of great opposition, with continued encouragement by Spirit-inspired prophets, the temple was completed.

As we struggle with the often discouraging, meager results of our own best efforts to build our churches and persuade a disinterested culture about Jesus, it's time to take a fresh look at a better way. Jesus told the disciples not to leave the city until they were empowered by the "gift of the Father" (see Luke 24:49). We must become desperate for a new wind of the Spirit. Sailing is better than rowing!

WAITING FOR THE WIND

I hate waiting. It is by any measure one of my least favorite things in life. I get impatient waiting in line at the supermarket. I get impatient waiting at red lights, especially when there are no cars anywhere to be seen in the opposite direction! I hate waiting for someone who was supposed to meet me at Starbucks fifteen minutes ago. I just hate waiting, period. Perhaps you do too. Yet waiting is one of the most important lessons we have to learn if we are serious about being faithful and effective disciples of Jesus. It is this discipline of waiting on God's timing that tests every one of us. We are addicted to activity, to being busy, because we tend to feel that if we're not busy, we're not being productive.

When we are waiting, it may seem like nothing is happening, but waiting is definitely not a passive activity. Waiting is neither easy nor passive. It is hard work. It is during the work of waiting that we begin to struggle with questions like whether we have really heard from God. It is while we wait that we begin to wonder if maybe we missed God somewhere, or if maybe we have sinned in some way and got disqualified. After a few years of waiting, Abraham and Sarah began to doubt that God really meant He was going to give them their own son, so they hatched an abortive attempt to bring about God's promise in their own way by having Abraham sleep with Sarah's maid (Gen. 16:1-2).

Whenever God begins a significant work, waiting is almost always a part of the process for its unfolding and eventual fulfillment. King Saul failed the waiting test when Samuel the prophet told him to wait for his arrival, so he could make the offering to God before going to war with the Philistines (I Sam. 13). King David passed the waiting test when, after Samuel anointed him as king, he had to flee for his life and live like an outcast for years, before God finally had him appointed king over Israel.

Waiting on God's perfect timing was one of the things that made Jesus so effective, and what will make us effective. When given the news that Lazarus was deathly ill, Jesus waited for two more days before going to him (John 11:5-6). Because He waited for God's moment, and didn't react out of the pressure of the situation or out of a codependent reaction to please those who had been sent to get Him, Jesus experienced an incredible victory and God gained great glory.

If we are serious about learning to sail on the wind of the Spirit, we must submit to the discipline of becoming increasingly sensitive to God's timing. It is during these seasons of waiting that we subjugate our own willfulness and independence; that we begin to discover that real power doesn't come from our good ideas, busyness or strategies, but from the Spirit of God. One of the last bits of instruction Jesus gave to His disciples before ascending to heaven was, *"Do not leave Jerusalem, but **wait** for the gift My Father promised...in a few days you will be baptized with the Holy Spirit"* (Acts 1:4-5). What did they do? They waited. Waited and prayed, prayed and waited. And then the Wind came!

Learning to wait for God's timing honors the sovereignty of God. In other words, it's not all up to us. So much of where we are in life is simply a function of God's sovereign plan. The reason we haven't yet seen the fulfillment of what God has promised us is not necessarily because we've somehow failed or gone off course, or because we haven't gotten the "formula" right. Perhaps it simply isn't His time yet. God is God—He is always in control!

Waiting on God is not only important in the personal issues of life; it is also important in the context of ministry. For example, in training our church's ministry team, we teach them that when someone comes up for prayer after the service, they should not assume that what the person asks prayer for is necessarily the first thing God wants to address. They know that the first thing to do is to wait for a sense of leading from the Holy Spirit. God knows what the most important issues are in their lives, and if we learn to partner effectively with Him, we will be the most help to people.

This is exactly what Jesus did when a crippled man's friends lowered him through the roof and set him down in front of Jesus (Luke 5:17-26). Most of us (assuming we would even have enough faith to attempt to pray for the man's healing) would charge right in and begin to pray that God would heal his paralysis. But Jesus said, "Friend, your sins are forgiven." Only after the man was restored in his relationship with God did Jesus address the physical issue and heal the man. If we want to learn to sail with the wind of the Spirit, we must learn to see what God sees, hear what He's saying, and wait for the promptings of the Holy Spirit.

I used to love to watch a pastor named John Wimber during his "clinic times," when he would model ministry. Typically, after teaching from the bible, he would say something like, "Okay, now put your bibles and notes away. We're going to pray and invite the Holy Spirit, and He's going to come and begin to touch people." Then he would pray a simple prayer, inviting the Holy Spirit to come; and then he would wait. And wait. And wait.

The first time I saw him do this, he waited so long I was becoming fidgety and uncomfortable (remember, I hate to wait!). He would just pace on the stage and occasionally look out over the congregation. Then eventually, he would begin to share what the Lord was saying, and, inevitably, there was a fruitful time of ministry. If we're going to become truly effective in ministry, we have to learn to "dial down" our emotions (rather than getting hyped-up), get our spiritual antennas up, and wait patiently, until we sense God speaking. It may take longer than we like, but it's so worth it. Sailing is better than rowing!

LETTING GO

About eight years ago, a close friend and former member of our church, who had since moved from California to Texas, called me with what she believed was a "word from the Lord." Lois told me, "The Lord wants you to let go." Then she added, "You're working too hard."

I've always believed in the value of hard work. I believe in the Judeo-Christian work ethic, and that we should see our work as a noble calling. But I've always guarded against becoming a workaholic; I've observed my "Sabbaths," taking Mondays off and even napping when possible during my workday, because I'm in this for the long haul. So when Lois told me I was working too hard, I didn't understand. And what was this about "letting go"? Let go of what?

I'm a little slow ("little" would be an understatement!), because it's taken me eight years to begin to understand what "letting go" means. But I've come to believe it's one of the most important lessons God wants to teach us, and it's vital if we're serious about learning to minister in the power of the Holy Spirit. It has to do with learning to switch gears. Because we are unable to control the wind (that's God's arena), we must work diligently to the best of our ability in the absence of wind (what I call "rowing"), learn to discern when the wind begins to blow, then switch to "sailing" by letting go of the oars and lifting the sails. What I mean is this: When the Spirit begins to initiate ministry of some kind—an unexpected encounter, a burst of inspiration, inner impressions or "pictures," etc.—we must learn to pay attention, to "let go" of our agenda, schedule, other priorities, and follow His lead. It was this holy flexibility that made Jesus and the first disciples so effective. They knew how to detect the moving of the Spirit and made it their habit to respond…with wonderful results.

This is not a lesson that comes easily for Westerners like us. We have been marinated in the juices of a materialistic, scientific worldview for three centuries, since the so-called "Enlightenment," and we're much more comfortable with our binders of plans and strategies, and the support of technology. Obviously there is a place for these things, but for many of us, ministry today bears little resemblance to what was modeled for us by Jesus and the first-century Christians. What once was vibrant, powerful, and unpredictable has too often become stale, ineffective drudgery.

The issue is not whether effort is involved—all ministry requires effort. The issue is the *source* of the energy. How much of the energy is coming from us and how much energy is being provided by the Spirit? One of the clues is the effect ministry has on the ones providing it. When we are functioning on our own "steam," we tend to expend more energy and have less joy. When we have the wind of the Spirit behind our backs, we expend less energy and have more joy. When the 70 disciples returned from their mission, Luke tells us they *"returned with joy"* (Luke 10:17). There can be joy in ministry!

According to the Apostle Paul, in Second Corinthians 3, the ministry we're involved in is "the ministry of the Spirit," and is, by its very nature, "glorious." When we attempt to do the work of the Spirit in the power of our own energy (physical, emotional, or mental), ministry stops being glorious and becomes predictable and cumbersome.

FINDING THE FLOW

Popular Science, in one of its past issues, had an interesting article about a company that is designing huge kites to help pull cargo ships across the oceans. The idea was that these kites would be released from the ships and ascend to the air currents high above, where they would fly ahead of the ships and provide extra pull. It was estimated that these giant kites would cut energy and fuel costs by at least one-third.

In much the same way as these air currents high above, there is a "flow" of energy that the Holy Spirit provides, faintly discernible much of the time, but thankfully more obvious some of the time. We can learn to detect these divine breezes, and, in doing so, become more fruitful and less-exhausted partners with the Holy Spirit in the ministry of Jesus.

Lloyd Ogilvie, former pastor of Hollywood Presbyterian Church and chaplain of the U.S. Senate, relates the story of how he discovered this dynamic during a particularly challenging week:

> Exhaustion set in. While doing a television taping I realized the overload was making me less

than maximum. What was usually done with ease became arduous and difficult. Living on my own resources proved to be very inefficient. The business of the previous days had shortened my devotional time and the pressures had distracted me enough so that I didn't draw on the divine energy I usually find so sufficient through moment-by-moment prayer through each responsibility.

It was during this time that Ogilvie also experienced an electrical power failure at his house. He then goes on to relate how the Lord spoke to him:

> "My son, you were created to be a transmitter of me. You've blocked the flow of my spirit by attempting more in this week than I guided and set as priorities. You've had a power failure just like your house. To do my will effectively, you must depend on me and the flow of my power."[1]

I have experienced this many times in preparing my sermons. Often God will give me a burst of inspiration (usually during my times of prayer in the early morning), and I'll begin writing notes. At first the ideas will flow quickly, and the beginnings of an outline will form nicely. Then, before long, I'll start searching my mental "hard-drive" for more ideas or illustrations, and before I know it, usually within 15-30 minutes, the flow will slow to a trickle. That's when inspiration morphs into perspiration and the fun stops, usually without my even realizing it. That's what I'm talking about. That's when I've left the "flow" of the Spirit, like a bird veering away from the air current that was carrying it, and I begin to lose altitude.

Now I've learned that when that happens, I simply put down my notes and do something else until another time, when, hopefully, the wind will blow again. Or I simply stay put, return to the simplicity of meditating on Him and the knowledge of His love and goodness, quit trying to get a sermon, and often the inspiration returns. Don't misunderstand; I love diving into my reference books and commentaries, but if I can do this without losing my awareness of the Holy Spirit, there is usually a greater sense of inspiration and enjoyment.

Have you ever been in a plane when it hit an air pocket? You're flying along nicely, reading your book or taking a nap, when suddenly, "Thump!" The plane drops unexpectedly, the engines rev as the air around the plane changes composition, and everyone gets a little shaken up. That's what it feels like when you veer away from Spirit-given momentum and begin relying on your own resources.

Proverbs 3:5 says, *"Trust in the Lord with all your heart; do not depend on your own understanding"* (NLT). Another way of saying this is, "Depend on the Lord and on His resources, and don't depend on your own energy or intelligence." Isaiah 40:30-31 says, *"Even youths grow tired and weary, and young men stumble and fall; but those who hope in the Lord* [some translations read, 'wait on the Lord'] *will renew their strength. They will soar on wings like eagles; they will run and not grow weary, they will walk and not be faint."* What an amazing picture of those who find the "flow" of the Holy Spirit; like eagles, they soar, carried by the momentum of a holy wind! Waiting, depending on God in a posture of faith, will reward us with the energy of God. Sailing is better than rowing!

The thing about sailing is that you are utterly dependent on wind. In that respect, rowing is easier, because you can, at least, do something! But if we are to cross the oceans of Kingdom adventure, rowing is definitely not the way to go. And if we are ever to become remotely as effective as Jesus was, we have to understand that there is simply no other way than being deeply and continually empowered by the same power that moved in and through Him—the power of the Spirit.

Understanding that Jesus intended for us to emulate Him is the starting point. But that understanding must develop within us a desire for the Holy Spirit to transform and empower us, to produce fruit and activate gifts. And, ultimately, that desire must be fanned into a flame of passionate desperation, fueled by an unshakable confidence that He will do it.

ENDNOTE

1. Lloyd Ogilvie, *Praying With Power* (Ventura: Regal Books, 1983), p. 90.

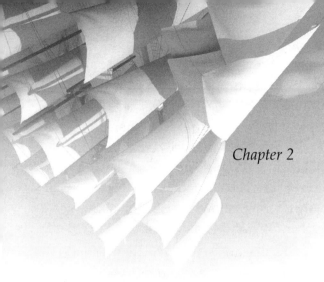

Chapter 2

WHO IS THIS PERSON?

"The Spirit gives life; the flesh counts for nothing. The words I have spoken to you are spirit and they are life."
John 6:63

One evening, after having spent some time teaching my eighth-grade daughter the various properties of math (the distributive property, associative property, substitution property, etc.), I was praying with her after tucking her in. In the course of my prayer I said something like, "…and Holy Spirit, surround her with Your presence." After I had prayed, Stephanie said, "Dad, is it okay to pray to the Holy Spirit?" I replied, "Well, is the Holy Spirit God?" To which she immediately said, "Yes." Then I said, "Is it okay to pray to God?" She thought for a moment and said, "Oh, I get it, the substitution property of equality!"

This deliciously profound statement of Trinitarian theology from an eighth grader reveals something of the delightful surprises and exciting adventure that await us as we explore this mysterious and wonderful Person.

The first thing to establish about the Holy Spirit is that He is, indeed, God. That has been firmly decided over centuries of church history and theological reflection. It is also enshrined in some of our most endearing hymns, such as "Holy, Holy, Holy"—which ends, "God in three persons, blessed trinity." How about the Doxology: "Praise God from whom all blessings flow. Praise Him all creatures here below. Praise Him above ye heavenly host. Praise Father, Son, and Holy Ghost."

What? Praise the Holy Ghost? Can we really do that? I mean, all believers have no problem praising God, and most believers are comfortable praising Jesus, but think about it—don't you get just a little uncomfortable with the idea of praising the Holy Spirit? When was the last time you did that? In fact, when was the last time you even spoke to the Holy Spirit?

One of my favorite choruses in the 1970's went like this: "Praise You, Father; bless You Jesus; Holy Spirit, thank You for being here, being here, Lord." So addressing the Father, Son, and Holy Spirit is nothing new to most of us in our worship. Still, talking to the Holy Spirit without the support of music seems oddly strange to many of us.

Jesus made it clear that it was a good thing for Him to leave and for the Holy Spirit to come. In John 16:7, He said, *"I tell you the truth: It is for your good that I am going away. Unless I go away, the Counselor will not come to you; but if I go, I will send Him to you."* Whenever Jesus said, "I tell you the truth" (or "verily, verily" in the King James Version), He was emphasizing something very important that He didn't want the listeners to miss. He was saying, "Guys, listen up. Pay attention to what I'm telling you. I know you don't want Me to leave. I know you don't understand, but trust Me—the next step in My plan for the world is vital: There's a new chapter about to unfold, and your place in destiny hinges on Me sending the Holy Spirit. He will enable you to take what I've begun and fill the world with the message and the power of the Kingdom."

One of the great mysteries of the Trinity is how the Father, Son, and Holy Spirit can be one, yet three distinct Persons. But it's precisely this mystery that draws us deeper into God, as we commit ourselves to a lifetime of adventure in discovering more about each of them. Each is God, yet each one is different from the other.

I understand that this can all be a little confusing. Trying to grasp the concept of "God in three Persons" has been a challenge to believers throughout the centuries, and has been the subject of many long theological debates. One day, while I was praying, I said, "Lord, sometimes I get a little confused about which one of You to address." And immediately I heard Him say back to me, "Just think of Us as one." Well, I know that sounds very subjective, but you've got to admit, it is sound biblically!

Luke used the terms "Holy Spirit" and the "Spirit of Jesus" interchangeably in Acts 16:6-7. First he says they had been *"kept by the Holy Spirit from preaching the word in the province of Asia."* Then, in the very next verse, he goes on to add, *"When they came to the border of Mysia, they tried to enter Bithynia, but the Spirit of Jesus would not allow them to."*

I have long maintained that the ministry of the Spirit and the ministry of Jesus are inseparable. When the presence of the Holy Spirit is palpable in a gathering, and people are powerfully touched, encouraged, or healed, it doesn't take long to realize that those are exactly the kinds of things Jesus always did in scripture—He touched, healed, and encouraged all who came to Him. And when the Holy Spirit is powerfully present, invariably Jesus is praised and God is glorified.

Some people are concerned that all of this focus on the Holy Spirit detracts from the centrality of Jesus. But I think this is, to a large extent, an unfounded fear. Jesus said that the Holy Spirit would testify about Him (John 15:26), and one way we recognize the Holy Spirit is exactly that: The Holy Spirit loves to exalt Jesus! So when He's present in a gathering, we invariably feel drawn to Jesus; we are moved to praise Jesus and to glorify Him as Lord and King. So in my prayer times and often throughout the day, I go back and forth, giving praise and thanking the Father, the Son, and the Holy Spirit.

I can just hear someone thinking, "But what if you thank the Spirit for something Jesus or the Father did, or vice versa?" Well, I figure they're big boys and can work it out up there! I mean, come on, do you really think there's any hint of competitiveness or confusion among the three members of the Trinity? Each of these wonderful three Persons is unique, yet so perfectly loves the others that They are all delighted at whatever praise comes to any of Them, and They are quick to overlook any imperfections in our praise.

THE JOY OF THE SPIRIT

As a pastor for over 30 years, I've been in many meetings where the presence of God has been manifested in unusual ways. Sometimes there's been a quiet sense of deep reverence, accompanied by lots of tears; at other times there's been a powerful anointing on the message, so that unplanned thoughts and words flow like a river, and I experience a feeling like electricity as I look over the congregation and know that the people are gripped by God's presence; at still other times, different people will begin to get messages from the Spirit in the form of pictures, phrases, scriptures, or thoughts. But some of the time, there is simultaneously a wonderful sense of lightheartedness and joy, often bubbling up into playfulness and laughter. (Please read my story under "Laughter" in Chapter 5.)

On several occasions, Jesus indicated that He wanted His followers to experience joy. I'll just mention two from the Gospel of John. In John 15:11, He said, "*I have told you this so that My joy may be in you, and that your joy may be complete.*" Notice, He said He wanted His joy to be in us. Since He is the purest, least inhibited, least contaminated, least fearful person in the universe, can you imagine what His joy feels like? Just think about it. It has to be better than any joy we can experience by ourselves! And He emphasized that He wanted our joy to be complete! That's the kind of joy I want to live in, and the Holy Spirit is the vehicle for that kind of living.

In John 17:13, in His famous prayer to the Father, Jesus said, *"I am coming to you now, but I say these things while I am still in the world, so that they may have the full measure of My joy within them."* The full measure!

The Holy Spirit has come to continue doing in us the things Jesus wanted done, and that includes experiencing the joy of Jesus. In Galatians 5:22, joy comes second only to love as the evidence of the Holy Spirit living in us (the "fruit" of the Spirit).

Lest you think joy is simply unnecessary "fluff" in the lives of believers, listen to what Nehemiah told the people when they had gathered to hear the Law: *"Go and enjoy choice food and sweet drinks, and send some to those who have nothing prepared. This day is sacred to our Lord. Do not grieve, for the joy of the Lord is your strength"* (Neh. 8:10). Joy has a strengthening effect on you. Obviously there are times when we need to weep and mourn, and we should never skip the crucial, healing phase of grieving our losses, or weeping in repentance, but this was not such a time, and Nehemiah had the insight to recognize it.

When the Holy Spirit is at work, joy happens! Joy has always been a hallmark of revival. Whether the revival in Hezekiah's day (II Chron. 30), the outpouring at Pentecost in Acts 2, Philip's revival in Samaria (Acts 8:5-8), the First and Second Great Awakenings, the Azusa Street revival, or the years surrounding the Jesus Movement in the 1970's, joy has always been generously present when the Spirit is poured out. When the Kingdom of God comes near, one of the things we should expect is for the Holy Spirit to give *"an inexpressible and glorious joy"* (I Pet. 1:8).

THE FELLOWSHIP OF THE HOLY SPIRIT

After the Holy Spirit came on the Day of Pentecost, one of the most visible signs that Jesus was powerfully at work was the intense closeness the new Christians felt toward each other. Jesus had prayed, in John 17:11, *"that they may be one as We are one."* Three times, in Acts 2:44-47, Luke uses the word "together." All the believers *"were **together** and had everything in common"*; they *"continued to meet **together**"*; and *"they broke bread...and ate **together**."* Here is the Spirit at work to answer the prayer of Jesus.

Over the years, one of the things I have noticed when God has been obviously at work in a group of believers, whether pastors or lay people, is that the level of fellowship intensifies. There comes a greater sense of transparency, trust, and love as they draw closer to the Lord and experience Him together. But I have also noticed that all of this comes, specifically, from the person of the Holy Spirit.

I have always enjoyed fellowship with pastors and leaders from different movements and denominations, but invariably, when I meet another pastor who shares a common experience of the Spirit, there is a quicker and deeper bond between us. It doesn't matter whether they are Pentecostal, mainline, independent, or Catholic. Once we discover that we both value the fullness of the Holy Spirit and His gifts, we simply click and become fast friends.

Just today, I had lunch with another pastor in a neighboring city. After spending some time in conversation catching up on each other's lives, the subject turned to my commitment to pursue the Holy Spirit with a new passion. Although I had no idea of his stance toward the work of the Spirit, he immediately perked up and our conversation seemed to take on a fresh and special quality. We were both powerfully encouraged by our mutual affection for the Person of the Holy Spirit and His work, and by the time our lunch ended, we were both as happy as two clams at high tide!

The best way to describe the effect of this time together is to say that our spirits were refreshed. I drove home greatly encouraged, smiling, even laughing and praising God! We had just experienced, what Paul referred to in Second Corinthians 13:14 as the *"fellowship of the Holy Spirit."*

Do you know someone who always seems to be "full of the Holy Spirit"? Do you know someone who always seems to stimulate you to draw closer to God, and who has the kind of effect on you that I just described? It might be a good idea to take them to lunch or breakfast, or have coffee at Starbucks, and see what the Holy Spirit does as you simply hang out together and talk about the Holy Spirit.

The Spirit truly is the great unifying factor of the Church. Paul was being very deliberate when he said, in Ephesians 4:3, *"Make every effort to keep the unity of the Spirit through the bond of peace."* Unity in individual churches, and also among churches is, specifically, a work of the Spirit, and wherever the Spirit is welcome, there exists greater potential for unity.

THE POWER OF THE SPIRIT

Kim lay there, flat on her back, in front of the church, overcome by the presence of the Holy Spirit. After about 20 minutes, she managed to pull herself to her feet, and then came up to me and told me that during her "floor time" the Lord had spoken to her about reconciling with her mom. She had not spoken to her mom in several years, so this was a significant moment for her.

Kim did, in fact, follow through with that clear message from God, and called her mom. Over the next few years they again became close, and when her mom was hospitalized for cancer at Cedars Sinai Hospital in Los Angeles, I had the privilege of praying with her for healing. It was one of those awkward times when I only had a couple of minutes to pray with her before the nurse came to begin a procedure, and I don't even remember what I prayed, but Kim called me a couple of days later to tell me the doctors could find no trace of cancer!

The thing I need to mention is that Kim's mom was not even a believer when God healed her! However, as great a miracle as her healing was, the Lord had an even greater miracle in store for her, as we visited her in a different hospital a few years later, and prayed with her to receive Jesus, just weeks before she died.

This entire series of events began with the Holy Spirit showing up in one of our services, and ministering to an area of deep emotional and relational pain in a daughter He loved. She may or may not have arrived at a similar place through months or years of professional counseling, but the Holy Spirit accomplished this loving and transforming work in a few minutes by His powerful touch.

I'm sure that many of you who are reading this right now can testify to other powerful works of the Spirit that you have seen. In fact, there is a growing litany of healings and miracles from all over the country, which, to me, is evidence that a wave is building which will bring a new Great Awakening.

Paul seemed to indicate that the gospel was only "fully proclaimed" when it included the power of the Holy Spirit. Read what he says in Romans 15:18-19:

> I will not venture to speak of anything except what Christ has accomplished through me in leading the Gentiles to obey God by what I have said and done—by the power of signs and miracles, through the power of the Spirit. So from Jerusalem all the way around to Illyricum, I have fully proclaimed the gospel of Christ.

This gospel of ours, at its very core, is a gospel of power. In Acts 10, when Peter was preaching to Cornelius and his friends, he told them, *"...God anointed Jesus of Nazareth with the Holy Spirit and power, and...He went around doing good and healing all who were under the power of the devil..." (Acts 10:38).* It was the power of the Spirit that enabled Jesus to heal and perform miracles.

In Fremont, California, a young man named Jack invited his friend, Dan, to church on a Friday night. Although Dan had been raised in church, he had gone astray for the past few years, but recently had begun praying again, and felt drawn back to church. At one point, the guest speaker stopped in the middle of his message and said, "There's a young man here tonight, who's been through a number of deep, personal things over the past few years, and has been running from God, but tonight God is calling him back." Almost before he could finish, Dan let out a groan, his hands shot up in the air as he stood to his feet and began gushing out a heavenly language at the top of his voice. By the time he had regained his composure a few minutes later, the entire church was on its feet praising God!

I am that Dan. That was my experience back in 1971, and I've never looked back. Many people come to Jesus through the testimony of a friend, or reading a book, or by an altar call or some kind of invitation, but in my case, I was apprehended by God through a powerful outpouring of the Holy Spirit. This was not the exception in New Testament times, but seems to have been a frequent experience, as signs and wonders and gifts of the Holy Spirit often accompanied the preaching of the word.

Paul tells us, in First Corinthians 2:4-5, *"My message and my preaching were not with wise and persuasive words, but with a demonstration of the Spirit's power, so that your faith might not rest on men's wisdom, but on God's power."* Don't you long to see more of the power of the Spirit to save men, women, and young people? Don't you yearn to experience more of His power for yourself?

The same Wind that came on the Day of Pentecost wants to blow afresh in your church and in your city! Jesus said, in Luke 11:13, *"If you, then, though you are evil, know how to give good gifts to your children, how much more will your Father in heaven give the Holy Spirit to those who ask Him!"*

THE SATISFACTION OF THE HOLY SPIRIT

There is simply nothing that satisfies our souls as deeply as the Holy Spirit. Many times we spend a few minutes in prayer or reading our bibles, experience a taste of God's blessing, and get up feeling pretty good about ourselves, ready to get on with our day. But there is a place that the Holy Spirit is inviting us into—a place where He wants to flow into the deepest recesses of our souls—into some pockets that haven't been saturated, perhaps for a long time, with His joy, peace, faith, and fullness. A fullness that brings an unshakable confidence that with God all things are possible; a fullness that changes our outlook and attitude; a fullness that reassures us that no matter what happens in our lives or in our country, God will accomplish His good purposes and plans for us, and that He loves us beyond anything we can imagine!

When my first daughter, Lindsey, was an infant, I used to get up in the middle of the night and feed her, because my wife, Jane, was working nights as a nurse. I would get some breast milk that Jane had stored in little baggies in the freezer, microwave them, and take the bottle into Lindsey's room. Then I would pick Lindsey up out of her crib and sit up with her in my bed, holding her in my left arm and feeding her the bottle with my right hand. The whole time she was nursing from the bottle, she would stare up into my eyes with her big, blue eyes wide open—a priceless time of bonding that I'll never forget. When she was full, she would slowly close her eyes, her little tongue still showing between her lips. It was a look of utter satisfaction! She was satiated—full and happy, ready to resume her peaceful sleep. That's what it feels like when you have drunk deeply from the Spirit of God. He satisfies!

THE LIFE OF THE SPIRIT

Jesus said, in John 6:63, *"The Spirit gives life; the flesh counts for nothing. The words I have spoken to you are Spirit and they are life."* That explains why, when people listened to Jesus, they were gripped, confronted, or transformed. But they never stayed the same, because the words that flowed from His lips came from another world. A few verses later, when the crowds began to desert Him, Jesus asked the Twelve, *"You do not want to leave too, do you?"* To which Peter replied, *"Lord, to whom shall we go? You have the words of eternal life"* (John 6:66-68). They were words of the Spirit.

In the next chapter of John, the chief priests and Pharisees sent the temple guards to arrest Jesus, but after listening to Jesus speak for a while, they went back. The chief priests and Pharisees asked them, *"Why didn't you bring Him in?"* They answered, *"No one ever spoke the way this man does"* (John 7:45-46). His words were "Spirit," and could not easily be dismissed.

In Romans 8:2, Paul referred to the Holy Spirit as the *"Spirit of life."* He was speaking as one who had experienced his own rebirth and filling of the Holy Spirit as Ananias laid hands on him. But he had also seen abundant evidence, over many years of ministry, that the Spirit was the life-giving force of the church, as men and women were radically saved, healed, and delivered, and as new churches were planted all over Asia.

When the Spirit is present in a person or in a church, He brings a power that transforms people. My constant prayer as a pastor is, "Lord, let this be a life-giving church." It's so easy to fall into what's cozy and familiar, to default into our routines and well-practiced agendas, but life flows when we deliberately follow the promptings of the Holy Spirit. When we commit to embracing the Spirit, our services may not always look polished or predictable, but people will find life, because the Spirit of Life is present.

When Jesus burst onto the scene, His competition was the stale, lifeless tradition of the Pharisees and Sadducees. *His* ministry, in contrast, was unpredictable, controversial, liberating, exciting, miraculous, and empowering because He had been anointed with the Holy Spirit at His baptism. Like champagne exploding from a bottle, the Jews could not restrain Him or limit His influence; they couldn't keep Him quiet or tame Him; they could only kill Him. And even then, the grave could not hold Him down!

When the Holy Spirit came on the Day of Pentecost, the Church was born, like a kicking, screaming baby, and quickly grew into a force that would overwhelm the Roman Empire. And over the centuries since then, despite opposition, persecutions, and scandals, the Church continues to expand all over the world, because, in the final analysis, it is a creation of the Spirit and has an eternal destiny.

Some years ago, a new church was planted in our city. I knew a lady who was part of the church plant, and we had numerous conversations about the Holy Spirit and His gifts. Unfortunately, when she approached the pastor and leaders about the gifts of the Spirit, they came down hard and made it clear that they would never allow the "charismatic" gifts in their church. A few days later I had a dream that a woman was driving a car, and a thick plastic bag was being pulled tightly over her head, suffocating her. I awoke with the distinct impression that the Lord had spoken to me about this new church, which was, like the woman in the dream, being suffocated by not allowing the Holy Spirit to work in the church. Within a few short months, the church plant failed, and the pastors left town. The Spirit is the life of the Church. It is costly to say "no" to the Holy Spirit!

THE MYSTERY OF THE SPIRIT

Whether you call yourself Evangelical, Pentecostal, Charismatic, Catholic, or Orthodox, you have been taught to believe that God exists eternally in three Persons: Father, Son, and Holy Spirit. You have also been taught that they are coequal, and the same in substance, but existing in distinct persons. Yet, in spite of two thousand years of theological reflection, so much mystery still surrounds the person of the Holy Spirit.

Mystery. That is something we in the Western world are uncomfortable with. We are addicted to finding answers and resolving discrepancies. Our scientific, rationalistic worldview has conditioned us to believe that the human mind can solve all mysteries. Thankfully, one of the blessings of this post-modern age is the realization that the modern age, which is passing into history, has not been able to provide satisfying answers to some of the most important questions of life, and that it is okay to live with some degree of apparent contradiction and irresolution, some level of mystery. In that way we are becoming more like the Christians in the first few centuries, when people were able to hold what appear to be opposing truths in tension (such as the sovereignty of God and the free will of man).

Yet, even though the Holy Spirit remains the most mysterious person of the Trinity, He has revealed enough of Himself in scripture so that we can know Him and engage in the exciting adventure of working in partnership with Him. My intent, here, has not been to unravel all of the controversy or to answer all of the questions surrounding the theology of the Holy Spirit—there are much more capable minds that have tackled that—but to bring enough clarity to help us move forward effectively in doing the works of Jesus. Following is a biblical survey of the work and ministry of the Holy Spirit, along with some observations about how we can live in a condition of Spirit-fullness:

1. In the Old Testament, the Spirit came only upon selected people.

For example, the Spirit imparted gifts of artistic creativity. In Exodus 31:1-5, we are told:

> ...The Lord said to Moses, "See, I have chosen Bezalel son of Uri, the son of Hur, of the tribe of Judah, and I have filled him with the Spirit of God, with skill, ability and knowledge in all kinds of crafts—to make artistic designs for work in gold, silver and bronze, to cut and set stones, to work in wood, and to engage in all kinds of craftsmanship."

The Spirit also came upon Samson and gave him supernatural strength. In Judges 14:6 we read, "*The Spirit of the Lord came upon him in power so that he tore the lion apart with his bare hands....*"

David's life was dramatically changed after the Holy Spirit came on him, following his anointing by Samuel. We are told in First Samuel 16:13, "*So Samuel took the horn of oil and anointed him in the presence of his brothers, and from that day on the Spirit of the Lord came upon David in power.*" Immediately, in the next verses, we see God's favor on him as David is being enthusiastically recommended to Saul, the king, and the following chapter records his historic victory over Goliath. Many other victories would follow, culminating in David becoming the greatest king in the history of Israel and Judah. What a difference the Holy Spirit made in the life of David!

2. The prophets promised that a time would come when God would pour out His Spirit upon *all* of His people.

In the course of prophesying about the future destruction of Israel because of her rebellion, Isaiah promised that there would follow a time of restoration and divine blessing. The focal point of this blessing would be the outpouring of God's Spirit. *"For I will pour water on the thirsty land, and streams on the dry ground; I will pour out My Spirit on your offspring, and My blessing on your descendants"* (Isa. 44:3).

Ezekiel echoed this theme of restoration and the outpouring of God's Spirit: *"'I will no longer hide My face from them, for I will pour out My Spirit on the house of Israel,' declares the Sovereign Lord"* (Ezek. 39:29).

But the most quoted passage is from Joel 2:28-29, where the prophet, after promising that God would *"repay* [them] *for the years the locusts have eaten,"* went on to declare:

> *And afterward, I will pour out My Spirit on all people. Your sons and daughters will prophesy, your old men will dream dreams; your young men will see visions. Even on My servants, both men and women, I will pour out My Spirit in those days.*

As we know, Peter quoted from this passage on the Day of Pentecost, and affirmed that the Pentecostal outpouring was a fulfillment of Joel's prophecy (Acts 2:16-21).

3. Jesus Himself was empowered by the Holy Spirit and emphasized the role the Spirit would play in the lives of His followers.

After Jesus was baptized by John in the Jordan River, we are told that the Holy Spirit descended upon Him in the form of a dove (Luke 3:22) and that after His time of testing in the desert, He returned *"in the power of the Spirit"* (Luke 4:14). The incredible ministry of Jesus that follows throughout the gospels is a commentary, an "unpacking" of the implications of this profound empowerment.

What Jesus experienced through the Holy Spirit was to become the model, the template, for each of His followers. On the last and greatest day of the Feast of Tabernacles, Jesus stood up and said in a loud voice, *"If anyone is thirsty, let him come to Me and drink. Whoever believes in Me, as the Scripture has said, streams of living water will flow from within him"* (John 7:37-38). John goes on to explain in verse 39, *"By this He meant the Spirit, whom those who believed in Him were later to receive."* An obvious reference to the river of life in Ezekiel 47, this is one of Jesus' most powerful and unambiguous statements about the life-giving function of the Holy Spirit in and through His followers.

The last thing Jesus told His disciples, before ascending to heaven, was that they were not to do anything until they had received the power of the Holy Spirit. In Acts 1:4-5 He instructed them (Luke says He "commanded" them), *"...Do not leave Jerusalem, but wait for the gift My Father promised, which you have heard Me speak about. For John baptized with water, but in a few days you will be baptized with the Holy Spirit."* Then in verse 8, He continued, *"...you will receive power when the Holy Spirit comes on you; and you will be My witnesses in Jerusalem, and in all Judea and Samaria, and to the ends of the earth."*

4. The early Christian leaders understood the necessity of being filled with the Holy Spirit.

When the young and growing church in Jerusalem was experiencing its first administrative crisis, the apostles called the people together and said, *"Brothers, choose seven men from among you who are known to be full of the Spirit and wisdom. We will turn this responsibility over to them..."* (Acts 6:3). The interesting thing about this is that these people were not primarily going to be concerned with preaching or church planting, or healing the sick, but with administration—a function that we don't necessarily think of in terms of requiring the fullness of the Spirit. In light of this passage, some of us may need to rethink that.

Another interesting situation occurs as the church begins to expand beyond the confines of Jerusalem and Judea, northward into Samaria. We are told:

> *When the apostles in Jerusalem heard that Samaria had accepted the word of God, they sent Peter and John to them. When they arrived, they prayed for them that they might receive the Holy Spirit, because the Holy Spirit had not yet come upon any of them; they had simply been baptized into the name of the Lord Jesus. Then Peter and John placed their hands on them, and they received the Holy Spirit* (Acts 8:14-17).

Paul's own radical conversion required that he be filled with the Holy Spirit. In Acts 9:17 we read:

> *Then Ananias went to the house and entered it. Placing his hands on Saul, he said, "Brother Saul, the Lord—Jesus, who appeared to you on the road as you were coming here—has sent me so that you may see again and be filled with the Holy Spirit."*

Jesus Himself had made it explicitly clear to Ananias that, in addition to needing his eyesight restored, Paul needed to be filled with the Spirit.

Finally, when Paul encountered a group of disciples in Ephesus, his first question was, *"Did you receive the Holy Spirit when you believed?"* When they confessed ignorance about the Holy Spirit, he quickly brought them up to speed, laid hands on them, and the Spirit came upon them (Acts 19:1-6).

In his book, *Paul, the Spirit, and the People of God*, Gordon Fee makes this statement about Paul's attitude toward the Holy Spirit:

> One reads Paul poorly who does not recognize that for him the presence of the Spirit as an experienced and living reality, was the crucial matter for Christian life, from beginning to end."[1]

5. The Filling of the Holy Spirit is both initiatory and continual.

There are five occasions in the book of Acts when new believers were described as being filled with the Holy Spirit for the first time (Acts 2:4; 8:14-19; 9:17-18; 10:44-46; 19:6). All five of these occasions were accompanied by observable phenomena—either speaking in tongues, prophecy, or other external signs not explicitly described. In other words, they and those around them knew that there had been an in-breaking of God's power.

Even though all believers in Christ have the Holy Spirit within them (Rom. 8:9), in Ephesians 5:18 we are urged to continue being filled with the Spirit. (In this passage, Paul uses the Greek tense that denotes continual action—literally, "be being filled.") Even the first disciples, not long after experiencing the dramatic outpouring of the Spirit at Pentecost, had their own refilled, as we read in Acts 4:31.

Why do we need to be filled and refilled with the Spirit? The short answer is, we leak! The daily grind of our lives and our spiritually hostile environment have a way of sapping our strength and draining us of Spirit-fullness, forcing us to be perpetually dependent on God. Beyond that, it is simply not God's best plan for us that we live only on memories and stories of past experiences, but that God's work in and through us always is fresh, new, wonderfully unpredictable and gloriously powerful!

6. How to be filled with the Holy Spirit

Repent

At Pentecost, at the conclusion of Peter's message to the crowd, they said, *"Brothers, what shall we do?"* to which Peter replied, *"Repent and be baptized...and you will receive the gift of the Holy Spirit"* (Acts 2:38). Although, in context, this was addressed to first-time believers, I have found, in my own experience, that whenever the Holy Spirit shows me an area in my life that I need to change, after I do repent, there is a new experience of God's grace and power. It is always true that the more we turn from those things that displease God and toward those things that are consistent with the character of Jesus, the more we make room for the Holy Spirit.

[The next two action items, which will help us to be filled with the Spirit, are both contained in Luke 11:9-13.]

Ask (Pray)

In this chapter, Jesus has just told the parable of the man who has a desperate neighbor pounding on his door at midnight for some food to share with his own unexpected guest. The point of the parable is the power of persistent prayer, and the verbs Jesus uses are all in the Greek tense that denotes continual action, as in "keep asking, keep seeking, keep knocking." Scripture is full of examples of men and women who refused to take "no" for an answer, and, as a result, obtained the blessing they were seeking from God. Developing the habit of prayer, including frequent, short prayers throughout the day, as well as occasions of extended prayer, sometimes with fasting, is one of the best ways to be filled, and to stay filled with the Spirit.

Believe

Jesus made clear in this passage that our confidence that God will answer our prayer for the Holy Spirit is rooted in the very nature of God as a good and loving father. Listen closely to what he says:

> *Which of you fathers, if your son asks for a fish, will give him a snake instead? Or if he asks for an egg, will give him a scorpion? If you then, though you are evil, know how to give good gifts to your children, how much more will your Father in heaven give the Holy Spirit to those who ask Him!* (Luke 11:11-13).

Our God delights in giving good gifts to His children! When you ask (persistently) for the Holy Spirit to fill you, you can be most assured that God will answer.

Immerse yourself in an environment rich in the presence of the Holy Spirit.

One of the things that has frustrated many pastors is the habit of some Christians to go running after every new revival, while neglecting the daily and often less flashy, mundane responsibilities to their families, church, and community. Often, these "hallelujah hobos" seem infatuated with every new spiritual fad that comes along, or with every new church that pops up in the area.

Having said that, there is something to be said for the kind of spiritual thirst that stops at nothing to drink from a genuine well of the Holy Spirit's refreshing and empowering presence. Some of the more significant moments in my pilgrimage have come as a result of traveling, sometimes great distances, to a place that I heard from credible sources was "the real thing," or to spend time with a person who had more of what I wanted. I have found that the Holy Spirit's blessings really can be transferred by osmosis and impartation.

What I'm not suggesting is that you assume you should leave a church just because the Spirit doesn't seem to be powerfully present, and to find a more "lively" one, but that you assume you should stay unless God confirms otherwise over a long period of time. (How can we transform what we leave?)

I recently met a friend who had prayed for years about leaving his church out of frustration about this issue, but had never sensed God giving him permission (ah, yes, getting God's permission—now there's a concept that's foreign to our consumerist culture!). Anyway, he finally asked the pastor if he would mind if he started a group for those wanting to experience more of the Spirit in their lives, and the pastor agreed. Now there are hundreds of men attending this group regularly, including the pastor! The Holy Spirit wants to come to thirsty churches!

Give yourself away.

The old illustration about the Dead Sea being that way because it has no outlet certainly holds true when it comes to the importance of ministry. One of the best ways to keep being filled with the Spirit is to find ways to minister to others. And finding ways to minister in pairs or groups increases both the joy and the impact, especially when ministry is extended to those outside the church. If you only seek greater fullness of the Spirit to satisfy your own appetite, you will soon become ingrown and of little use in the Kingdom. But if you grow in your desire to help others through His power, God will delight in giving you more and more of His Spirit. He really cares about people, and one of His great, unchanging goals is to grow this love for others in us.

ENDNOTE

1. Gordon Fee, *Paul, the Spirit and the People of God* (Peabody, MA: Hendrickson, 1996), p. xiii.

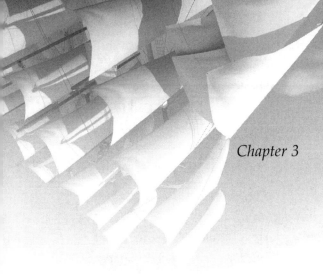

Chapter 3

YOU CAN DO THE WORKS OF JESUS

"I tell you the truth, anyone who has faith in Me will do what I have been doing." John 14:12

Neverland ………

Treasure Island…………..

Camelot…………...

Narnia

These are the places that occupy our childhood thoughts and captivate our imaginations, because these are the places of adventure, where everything is possible, and where good always triumphs over evil. How many of us, as kids, imagined that we were hunting for hidden treasure, sure that just over the next hill, or under the next rock, we would find a fortune in gold and jewels? How many of us imagined that we were living in the times of castles and lords, and that we were the kings or queens, surrounded by servants and ruling with power?

Yet as we grow up, and are introduced to the real Kingdom of God, we usually assume we have traded the beauty, innocence, and wonder of those places for something less excit-ing, something less stimulating, less captivating. But would God do that to us? Would God really give us imaginations and dreams that cannot be matched by the reality of what He has for us? Paul didn't think so. In Ephesians 3:20-21, he said

*Now to Him who is able to do **immeasurably more than all we ask or imagine**, according to His power that is at work within us, to Him be glory in the church and in Christ Jesus throughout all generations, for ever and ever! Amen.*

Many of us live Christian lives that are not too different from the drab black and white TV pictures of our parents' gen-eration, but the Kingdom that we are introduced to in scripture is painted in brilliant high-definition colors. This is a place where glorious angels fight for us, where rivers magically appear in the desert and turn the barren landscape into a lush garden. This is a land where the mountains burst into song and the trees of the field clap their hands, where the children of God are finally revealed in their glorious splendor, while all creation celebrates! This is the place where men walk on water, and every sickness and disease is banished, where every bondage is broken and every potential-inhibiting dysfunction is shattered. This is the land where dreams come true; where the poor are enriched and the lonely embraced into healthy families. This is the place where evil is destroyed, temptation disappears, and all tears are wiped away.

God experiences great pleasure in seeing His children blown away with joy and wonder as they do things they never thought possible. When the 70 new believers returned from their first mission of healing and casting out demons, Luke tells us that Jesus was *"filled with the joy of the Holy Spirit"* (Luke 10:21 NLT). Imagine how He felt when Peter walked on water! My hope is that, as you read this book, you will become more and more disenchanted with the "normal" life and will step out of your boat and follow Jesus into the wonderfully unpredictable and rewarding world of Kingdom life and ministry.

LEARNING TO HEAR

In February of 2005, six of us, including my wife and our associate pastor, Mike Flynn, and his wife, Sue, and two others were in Uganda at the request of the Anglican Church, to conduct a healing conference. One day we were driving on a long, isolated stretch of road between towns, surrounded by nothing but banana trees and miles and miles of red dirt, when the van began overheating. We eventually made our way to a dilapidated service station, where the man in charge told us our engine had blown a head gasket, which would take hundreds of dollars and five or six hours to repair. This was not good! We didn't have either the time or the money to spare, but neither did we want to break down in the middle of Uganda, with no town in sight for a hundred miles or more. We talked for some time with each other about what to do.

Finally, Mike reminded us of the scripture in Colossians 3:15: *"Let the peace of Christ rule in your hearts...."* He shared with us that the word used for "rule" was from the word for umpire, and that the Spirit often made this real to him by giving him a physical sign, which manifested itself through either a sense of calm or a sense of disturbance beneath his sternum. Now, obviously, New Testament scholars will probably want to parse this interpretation and the application of this verse, but nevertheless we, collectively, did indeed arrive at a sense of peace about going on with our trip. So we simply filled the radiator with fresh water and coolant and went on to the conference in the city of Mbarara without further incident.

I have "heard" the audible voice of God perhaps four times in my life that I recall. Actually, only two of those times were definitely audible; the other times were inner impressions, so sudden and so clear that they had the impact of being audible words from God. I share with you now one of those times I was so deeply spoken to by God that it has marked my soul like nothing else I can remember.

It was early in the morning, about six o'clock or so, and I was sitting on the porch of a beautiful bed and breakfast in Ballard, a small town about an hour north of Santa Barbara, California, where a group of us, pastors and wives, had gathered for a leaders' retreat. As I sat there in the cool stillness of the early morning, the dew still on the grass, with only the sound of a bird or two nearby, I found myself wondering at the magnificence of God's creation as I stared at the rose just in front of the porch railing. Softly I said, "Lord, it's so beautiful!" And immediately I heard Him say, "It's nothing compared to what I'm doing in you!"

That simple, yet exquisitely loving statement was so unexpected and so unlike anything I could ever imagine thinking about myself, that I was stunned and deeply moved at the same time. And in the five or six years since then, it still has the power to move me more than anything in my recent memory. That Jesus loves me in such a personal way, that He is shaping my life and filling it with significance, beauty, and value, makes sense of all the pain, failure, and struggle of the past fifty-plus years and gives me profound hope and faith for the future.

Theologians can explain those same truths to us, the truths about God fulfilling His purposes for us, and that our lives have significance, and we can gain a degree of insight into them from our own reading of scripture, but it's simply not the same as having the Author Himself speak to us in this deeply personal way. (Please understand, in no way is this intended to minimize the absolute importance of scripture—I have always maintained that one of the most powerful ways God speaks to us is from His written word.)

Now imagine God speaking to you in a similar way about someone else, to share with them for the purpose of touching their lives, bringing greater healing, empowerment, and joy to them than anything most of us have seen in our Christian experience. Imagine God regularly using you as a conduit for His life-transforming word. This kind of thing is not "fluff" or "charismania," but part of the essence of biblical and historic Christianity.

This is what Jesus did when He was first introduced to Peter and said to him, *"You are Simon, son of John. You will be called Cephas, which, translated, means Peter or 'Rock'"* (John 1:42). Or what He did when He saw Nathaniel and said to him, *"Here is a true Israelite, in whom there is nothing false"* (John 1:47). Or when He encountered the woman at the well and said to her, *"You have had five husbands, and the man you now have is not your husband"* (John 4:17-18), yet said it with no sense of judgment or rebuke and offered her the "living water" which could (and did) change her life forever.

You, too, can learn to hear God, both for yourself and for others. You, too, can learn to touch people with words of Spirit-originated power, watching in grateful awe, as Jesus melts their hearts and heals their souls. It is the message of the New Testament that these powers of the coming age of the Kingdom have already arrived, in measure, through the gift of the Spirit.

But how, exactly, do we learn to hear God? I've found that I hear God best early in the morning, or when I take time to seek Him through prayer and fasting, and especially when I get out of town to a place where I can be undistracted. But for starters, just ask Him for ears to hear. That is a prayer He loves to answer.

In their book, *The Rabbit and the Elephant*, Tony and Felicity Dale list a few basic ways that are a great beginning. Tony says that the most common way God speaks to us is probably through our thoughts, and relates the following story:

> Felicity used to do a lot of counseling. In order to reduce the time spent in counseling, she would

pray prior to each session and then write down the thoughts that came into her mind about that person's situation. Thoughts often seemed to come from left field, but she wrote them down anyway. About 85 to 90 percent of the time, when Felicity went back and reviewed her notes, the things that she had written down—the things that she thought the Lord had shown her—were accurate. On one occasion, a girl with depression came for counseling, and the Lord had already told Felicity that the girl's father had abused her. So it took only two questions to find the root of her depression: "How was your relationship with your father?" and "Did he abuse you in any way?"…That exercise taught Felicity to trust the Lord to speak to her through that "thought out of nowhere" as she prayed.[1]

IMAGINE

What would happen if someone in your church experienced a real miracle? I'm not talking about God healing someone's headache or sore elbow, but an indisputable miracle, like someone whom everyone knows is blind, and has been blind from birth, who's been sitting next to her seeing-eye dog in church every week, and someone lays hands on her and she's instantly healed and can see with 20/20 vision! Can you imagine the repercussions? The word would be out all over the community, and eventually the media would pick up the story. It would be on YouTube, and all over the country it would be the topic of conversation around water coolers, in lunchrooms and chat rooms, and over neighborhood fences.

Now imagine being part of a church where this kind of thing, and many other miracles and healings, happen on a regular basis. Imagine God moving in the hearts of people in the church to such a profound degree that they begin selling their vacation homes, investment properties, and extra cars and giving millions of dollars to the poor and to the church. Imagine people from the community flooding into the church because they've been so impressed with the love and power flowing from these ordinary people that they simply have to find out what's going on. Imagine hundreds, even thousands, of people in that city embracing Jesus as their Savior and Lord, being baptized, connecting into small groups, and growing strong in their relationship with God under the instruction of godly lay leaders and pastors. Imagine being caught up in this whirlwind of Spirit-inspired excitement, getting together every day in homes, at Starbucks, over lunch or dinners, or at school with others who are also experiencing the electric energy of this divine wave. Imagine church being more fun and exciting than any major league game or New Year's Eve party!

Sound far-fetched? But that's exactly the picture of the church given to us at the end of the second chapter of Acts:

> *Those who accepted his message were baptized, and about three thousand were added to their number that day. They devoted themselves to the apostles' teaching and to fellowship, to the breaking of bread and to prayer. Everyone was filled with awe, and many wonders and miraculous signs were done by the apostles. All the believers were together and had everything in common. Selling their possessions and goods, they gave to anyone as he had need. Every day they continued to meet together in the temple courts. They broke bread in their homes and ate together with glad and sincere hearts, praising God and enjoying the favor of all the people. And the Lord added to their number daily those who were being saved* (Acts 2:41-47).

The book of Acts continues with story after story of ordinary people, empowered by the Holy Spirit, doing extraordinary exploits in the name of Jesus, for the glory of God. We must recapture the treasure of the Holy Spirit's power promised to the Church by Jesus, and dust off the gifts that He has distributed and continues to give. The Church, which in many respects has been a "sleeping giant," must be awakened and mobilized to forcefully advance the Kingdom of God in a deteriorating world.

LEARNING TO SEE

Jesus could do nothing by Himself. That was His confession in John 5:19. Actually, what He said was, *"Very truly I tell you, the Son can do nothing by Himself; He can do only what He sees His Father doing, because whatever the Father does the Son also does."*

It's essential to understand that Jesus' ability to "see" what the Father was doing was a result of the Spirit coming upon Him. One of the earliest prophecies about Jesus is found in Isaiah 11:1-3, which foretold His coming as a descendent of Jesse and David. We read:

> *A shoot will come up from the stump of Jesse; from his roots a Branch will bear fruit. The Spirit of the Lord will rest on Him—the Spirit of wisdom and understanding, the Spirit of counsel and of power, the Spirit of knowledge and of the fear of the Lord—and He will delight in the fear of the Lord. He will not judge by what He sees with His eyes, or decide by what He hears with His ears....*

Jesus did not draw conclusions based on what He saw, or what people told Him. He did not react to situations based on predictable human responses. He had learned to be sensitive to a superior source of information—the Holy Spirit—and that is the real reason for His phenomenal effectiveness, and the key to what could be ours.

So, returning to what Jesus said in John 5:19, one of the lessons we need to master is to see what the Father is doing. In other words, we need to develop our spiritual eyesight, our spiritual discernment. This is one of the basic skills we have neglected over centuries of disuse, and which we must reclaim. How do we do this? Like all spiritual gifts, we develop this ability through desperation for effectiveness, by pursuing Jesus, by believing in the generosity and goodness of God, by a commitment to risk-taking, and by a passionate appreciation for the person and work of the Holy Spirit. Let me share with you a recent example of how it has worked for me.

One Sunday morning I began with a short teaching, followed by a reminder that we are all called to do the works of Jesus (John 14:12), and suggested we pray and invite the Holy Spirit to direct us in ministry. As I began to pray, I immediately saw (in my mind's eye) a picture of a foot. At the end of the prayer I asked, "Does anybody here have a problem with their feet?" First one hand went up, then another, and eventually eight people responded. I invited them to come forward for prayer and had them stand up on the stage, facing the congregation. Then I asked for those who wanted God to begin using them to heal the sick to come forward and pray for them. I coached them through a simple healing prayer model, and interacted with the congregation about what the Holy Spirit seemed to be doing in each of the people being prayed for. At the end of the prayer time, I invited any of the eight who had noticeably experienced any degree of healing to share with the congregation, and several did so. Their sense of having been touched by God was obvious, as was the increase of faith throughout the church.

The important thing to know is that I am definitely not the only person in our church to "see" these spiritual pictures. We have many lay people who "see" these kinds of pictures regularly, and I'm convinced that every believer in Jesus has the potential to activate this and many other gifts of the Holy Spirit. He has invited us to ask!

What enabled Jesus to change the world in three short years was not the fact that He was God in the flesh. He had left behind, in heaven, all divine rights and inherent super-powers, and had become fully human. It is essential that we understand and embrace this truth. What enabled Jesus to change the world was the power of the Holy Spirit, which came upon Him at His baptism. When Peter was introducing Cornelius and his friends to Jesus, he said, "...*God anointed Jesus of Nazareth with the Holy Spirit and power, and...He went around doing good and healing all who were under the power of the devil, because God was with Him*" (Acts 10:38).

If we seriously believe that Jesus intended for us to imitate Him and do the things He did, we must begin to see *His* life and ministry as *our* example. Jesus was not only the savior of the world; He was and is our model for life and ministry. He apprenticed ordinary men and women, commissioning them to heal the sick, cast out demons, and raise the dead—first the twelve, then seventy more generic disciples (Luke 10:1). We need a fresh approach to the gospels and Acts: Not just as "bible study," but also as a training manual. In that way we will discover what made Jesus and the first disciples so effective, and how we can emulate their success.

Peter and other disciples understood clearly that Jesus' mission had been handed off to them—and to us—just as in a relay race a runner hands off a baton to the next runner. They had obviously learned their approach to ministry under the tutelage of Jesus; they had taken over the baton, and ran their leg of the race well.

For example, Mark described how Jesus took only Peter, James, and John into the home of Jairus, whose daughter had died (Mark 5:37-43). Then they watched as Jesus put all the noisy mourners out of the room and raised the girl to life. It's profoundly amusing to read Acts 9:40 and to see Peter do exactly the same thing in his raising of Tabitha from the dead. First he put the mourners out of the room, then prayed, turned toward the dead woman and told her to get up. He had learned ministry by observing Jesus, he had been empowered by the same Spirit as Jesus, and now he continued in the footsteps of Jesus. High five, Peter!

MYSTERY, IDENTITY, AND DESTINY

"In the beginning was the Word, and the Word was with God, and the Word was God" (John 1:1). The very choice of those words by the Holy Spirit, as He inspired the prologue of John's gospel, should tell us something of the unfathomable mystery of Jesus' true glory and identity. As much as the gospels and the other writings of the New Testament reveal about Jesus, there remains even more about Him that we haven't fully explored, and perhaps never can, this side of eternity. But if we would only take the time to explore as much of Him as scripture reveals, especially those mysterious, tantalizing glimpses given to us in passages such as the one above, or in Hebrews 1, we may find ourselves becoming preoccupied, wonderfully distracted from lesser pursuits, captivated by His beauty and power.

One of the reasons we should engage in such seeking, is that, in the pursuit of Jesus, in the discovery of all that He is, we find our true selves. The Spirit Himself said as much through the Apostle Paul, as he wrote the words of Colossians 3:3: *"...for you died, and your life is hidden with Christ in God."* It's as if God has the blueprint for our lives, all that He designed us to be and do, rolled up, sealed, and hidden in a vault called Jesus. As we discover the Person of Jesus—all He was in His pre-incarnate glory, all He was in the mission of His humanity, all He was in His post-resurrection body, and all He is now, as He sits at the right hand of the Father in eternal glory, we begin to discover our own glorious design and destiny as God's sons and daughters.

As we contemplate the amazing Son of God, we begin to see our true selves, created to be the image-bearers of God in this world, redeemed and restored to our rightful place as heirs of God and co-heirs with Christ. And we begin to see that we are called to be partners with Jesus, empowered by the same Spirit to be fellow-rescuers of a fallen planet.

We have been given both future glory and present power. We have been redeemed; we are being transformed; we will be glorified. We are each God's masterpiece, but a masterpiece with a purpose. Unlike Michelangelo's *David* or DaVinci's *Mona Lisa*, we are not designed to be on stationary display like static works of the Great Artist, but to reflect His glory in the daily course of our lives, to move gracefully through the world, speaking the words and doing the works of Jesus in the power of the Spirit.

My purpose in this brief overview is to show that our ministry in the power of the Holy Spirit is not intended to be something extra or esoteric, but is, in fact, a very part of our essence, our nature. The word theologians would use is "onto-logical." That is to say, it is part of our very being, our DNA.

Yet this power is not for us to employ independently. The power of the Holy Spirit is derivative. It flows out of a vital, ongoing relationship with Jesus. He said, *"If you remain in Me and I in you, you will bear much fruit"* (John 15:5). That simple statement of the intimacy that Jesus intended for each of us to experience with Him is perhaps the greatest key to doing the wonderful works He did. Mark tells us that Jesus *"appointed twelve that they might be with Him and that He might send them out to preach and to have authority to drive out demons"* (Mark 3:14-15). The order is important! Their first priority was simply to "be with Him." It was out of that intimacy that power would flow through them. The power was not only through impartation and commissioning; it was first through osmosis.

FROM PHARISEE TO FREEDOM

What a difference the Holy Spirit makes! Over the years I've seen stale, religious people transformed into fresh, exciting people-magnets by the power of the Spirit. I've watched luke-warm believers recapture their first love and embrace a new sense of adventure with Jesus. I've seen firsthand how entire churches have been revived with a new sense of mission and enthusiasm as the Holy Spirit has swept over them like Eze-kiel's life-giving river.

Paul had been trained as a Pharisee. He had been thor-oughly schooled in the scriptures of the Old Testament, and, like any good Pharisee, had memorized long passages, and could repeat them by heart. The problem was, even though these scriptures were inspired by the Holy Spirit, the way he and others like him used these scriptures resulted in bondage instead of freedom. And although they knew the scriptures, probably better than most of us today, they were blind to the reality of Jesus as the Son of God.

Then Paul had a life-changing encounter with the risen Jesus on his way to Damascus, was baptized by Ananias, filled with the Spirit, and embarked on an entirely new life and min-istry. His fascinating words in Second Corinthians 3:6 explain the difference between the "ministry of the letter" and the "ministry of the Spirit." Paul says, *"He has made us competent as ministers of a new covenant—not of the letter, but of the Spirit; for the letter kills, but the Spirit gives life."* It is obvious from this statement that it is possible to use the scriptures ("misuse" would be more accurate) in a way that results in spiritual bar-renness—even spiritual death.

Keep in mind, the scriptures of the Old Testament, which were so highly regarded by the Pharisees, were every bit as inspired by the Holy Spirit as the scriptures of the New Testa-ment. These were the same scriptures that Jesus referred to so often in His own ministry, yet when Jesus spoke them, they produced life, healing, and freedom; when the Pharisees spoke them, they produced bondage, guilt, and death. We should, then, infer that the same could be true of the New Testament scriptures: They can result either in bondage or freedom, depending on the person speaking them.

After explaining how superior the New Covenant is to the Old Covenant, Paul goes on to reveal this "Spirit" he is talking about. In verse 17, he says, *"Now the Lord is the Spirit, and where the Spirit of the Lord is, there is freedom."* By "Lord," he is referring to Jesus, and he is substantially equating Jesus with the Spirit ("the Lord is the Spirit"). What Paul is saying is that when we minister in the power and grace of the Spirit, we are, in fact, entering into the ministry of Jesus. And what was the ministry of Jesus like? One does not have to look far to find the answer. The gospels are filled with Jesus' powerful words and works.

The ministry of the Spirit (which is also the ministry of Jesus) combines the words of scripture with the powerful works of the Holy Spirit. Paul, and many later disciples, emulated the ministry of Jesus by powerfully quoting scripture and by working miracles in the name of Jesus through the power of the Holy Spirit. If we are to minister in the Spirit of Jesus, if we are to faithfully and accurately represent Him to the world, we must follow His example, speaking His words *and* doing His works.

At this point I believe it is important to provide an overarching perspective for any ministry characterized by signs and wonders. One of the criticisms I hear about some churches who are experiencing "renewal"-type phenomena is that they seem self-absorbed, content to simply "play" in their charismatic parties, with little regard to the needs of the lost community around them. It must be emphasized that the purpose for the power of the Spirit is to equip believers to help bring Kingdom transformation to unchurched people, cities, and nations. This includes doing *all* the works of Jesus: freeing people from the ravages of sin and bringing them into the wonderful freedom of the body of Christ, feeding the hungry, clothing the naked, imparting redemptive love and compassion to the emotionally bruised and hurting, contending for justice and mercy on all fronts, healing the sick, casting out demons, etc., with special emphasis on reaching out to the poor.

After the Spirit came on the Day of Pentecost, one of the first things the church did was to take care of the widows in the city of Jerusalem. It's no wonder that in those days the church enjoyed the favor of the community and grew dramatically. Being a missional people will help prevent the church from becoming introverted, irrelevant, and isolated from the culture. We will deal more with this topic in Chapter 11, "The Spirit and the Mission."

ENDNOTE

1. Tony and Felicity Dale and George Barna, *The Rabbit and the Elephant* (Carol Stream, IL: 2009), 49-50.

Chapter 4

Growing Bananas in Alaska

"With God all things are possible." Matthew 19:26

I lived in Zimbabwe until the age of eleven, and, along with a mini-vineyard my dad had planted, we grew a variety of tropical fruit—guavas, passion fruit, papayas, and bananas. The sub-equatorial climate, with its humidity and rainy season, was conducive to a range of interesting plants and fruit, including sugar cane, which we bought in six-foot lengths from vendors on the dirt roads. We would cut the cane into lengths of about eight inches, strip the hard covering, and chew the sugar cane on the inside, swallowing the sweet juice and spitting out the leftover pulp. (This probably helps to explain why so many African kids are a dentist's nightmare!)

We found similar fruit in the Hawaiian Islands. When Jane and I traveled to Kauai for our 25th anniversary, we had barely driven out of the airport when we began passing fields of sugar cane. Along with mangos, papayas, and guavas, we also enjoyed the best pineapples in the world!

One would not be surprised to find these kinds of fruit growing in Africa or Hawaii, but imagine getting out of a plane in Fairbanks, Alaska, barely a hundred miles from the Arctic Circle, and finding banana plantations or fields of pineapples! Imagine huskies pulling your sled through fields of guavas and mangos, while you waved at polar bears! Or picture yourself driving up to your Alaskan hotel in mid-winter, and instead of seeing nothing but snow and ice for miles around, you see people walking around in shorts and flip-flops, playing in the pool or sunbathing in 80-degree weather, lathered with sunscreen.

Of course, we know that scenarios such as the one above only occur in sci-fi movies, right? I mean, where else can you find a barren wasteland suddenly transformed into a lush garden? (Not that Alaska is a barren wasteland, for any Alaskans who may be reading this. I was referring specifically to the area around the Arctic Circle.) What would it take for that kind of radical transformation to happen? Nothing less than a climate change of historic proportions.

Actually, the prophet Ezekiel saw a similarly improbable scene unfold before his very eyes. Listen to how he describes it in Ezekiel chapter 47:

> The man [angel] *brought me back to the entrance of the temple, and I saw water coming out from under the threshold of the temple toward the east (for the temple faced east). The water was coming down from under the south side of the temple, south of the altar. He then brought me out through the north gate and led me around the outside to the outer gate facing east, and the water was flowing from the south side.*
>
> *As the man went eastward with a measuring line in his hand, he measured off a thousand cubits and then led me through water that was ankle-deep. He measured off another thousand cubits and led me through water that was knee-deep. He measured off another thousand and led me through water that was up to the waist. He measured off*

another thousand, but now it was a river that I could not cross, because the water had risen and was deep enough to swim in—a river that no one could cross. He asked me, "Son of man, do you see this?"

*Then he led me back to the bank of the river. When I arrived there, I saw a great number of trees on each side of the river. He said to me, "This water flows toward the eastern region and goes down into the Arabah, where it enters the Sea [the Dead Sea]. When it empties into the Sea, the water there becomes fresh. Swarms of living creatures will live wherever the river flows. There will be large numbers of fish, because this water flows there and makes the salt water fresh; so **where the river flows everything will live.** Fishermen will stand along the shore; from En Gedi to En Eglaim there will be places for spreading nets. The fish will be of many kinds—like the fish of the Great Sea... Fruit trees of all kinds will grow on both banks of the river. Their leaves will not wither, nor will their fruit fail. Every month they will bear, because the water from the sanctuary flows to them. Their fruit will serve for food and their leaves for healing."*

Just pause for a minute and reflect on this amazing picture. What Ezekiel sees is a stream, which flows from the temple and grows larger and larger the farther it moves into the desert, bringing life wherever it flows. Not only does it produce large amounts and varieties of marine life, but the land around the river becomes a tropical paradise, with "all kinds" of fruit growing in abundance! A desolate, barren wilderness is transformed into a beautiful, fruitful garden.

Jesus very likely had this famous Old Testament passage in mind, when, on the last and greatest day of the Feast of Tabernacles, He stood in the temple courts and said in a loud voice, "If *anyone is thirsty, let him come to Me and drink. Whoever believes in Me, as the Scripture has said, streams of living water will flow from within him."* Then John adds, *"By this He meant the Spirit, whom those who believed in Him were later to receive"* (John 7:37-39).

Jesus was saying that whoever puts their trust in Him will not only have their own spiritual thirst quenched, but they will also become a source of refreshment and life-transformation to others. What a beautiful picture: Believers in Jesus are people out of whom can flow life-giving streams, bringing transformation to individuals, churches, cities, and nations, by the power of the Holy Spirit!

There's another place in scripture where a garden like the one in Ezekiel is mentioned. This one is in Genesis chapter 2 and it's called "The Garden of Eden." We all know about the human tragedy that occurred as a result of the Fall: Man was banished from the garden, and all of his relationships were profoundly damaged—his relationship with God, with others, and with himself. But God, in His great love, did not abandon man to the desolate wilderness of his sin, but immediately set in motion His plan to redeem man and to restore his access to the "Garden," which will find its ultimate fulfillment in the future Kingdom of God.

Uganda is an example of what can happen when an entire nation is transformed by the Spirit of God. Under the brutal dictatorships of Milton Obote and Idi Amin, the nation suffered unimaginable pain, as thousands of men, women, and children were savagely killed. For years, no westerners dared to travel to this country because of the darkness and danger. But on our trip to Uganda a few years ago, we saw a completely different nation. There was stability, optimism, and a noticeable vibrancy in the people. Throngs of students in uniforms were everywhere, walking safely to their various schools; vendors were selling their goods in roadside stands and market squares, and the stores were doing a brisk business. There was animated conversation and laughter on streets and in neighborhoods throughout the capital of Kampala. Churches all over Uganda were full every Sunday, some of them several times during the day. In fact, the average-size church in Uganda has around 700 people in attendance (by comparison, the average-size church in the U.S. has about 70).

What caused this transformation? As related by some of the pastors, the people began crying out to God in desperation. Many would spend entire days and nights, hiding in the jungle, praying with deep groaning and tears for God to deliver their country. There have been so many miracles in the wake of this wind of the Spirit that they have been impossible to track, including hundreds of documented healings from AIDS.[1] Even the Anglican Church, which is several times larger than its counterpart in the U.S., the Episcopal Church, has seen many healings and miracles, along with the proliferation of other gifts of the Holy Spirit.

EXPECT THE "IMPOSSIBLE"

The story of Uganda is only one of many examples that could be presented as evidence that the Holy Spirit can transform cities and even entire nations. But beyond the historical evidence is the powerful testimony of Ephesians 3:20-21:

Now to Him who is able to do immeasurably more than all we ask or imagine, according to His power that is at work within us, to Him be glory in the church and in Christ Jesus throughout all generations, for ever and ever! Amen.

Our imaginations and dreams of revival, national renewal, and a worldwide harvest can sometimes seem fanciful and exaggerated, but here Paul is profoundly clear that even our most ambitious longings and desires are no match for God's power! He is always able to do *more* than anything we can imagine. And He does it through the power of His Spirit that is at work in us!

Jesus so often challenged, invited, and encouraged His followers to attempt what seemed humanly impossible (like walking on water or casting out the most stubborn demons). But even if He had never said or done any of those things, this verse, all by itself, should be sufficient encouragement for us to expect the impossible. If we can truly come to grips with the implications of this scripture, the transformation of our churches, cities, and nations would be patently within our reach. Read it over and over, slowly, and let its truth sink deep into your heart. God is able to do immeasurably more than anything you can ask or imagine!

On a fateful Sunday morning in 1988, our service took an unusual turn when several sobering prophetic words were shared. I knew the people giving them, and they weren't flakes, so I felt something was up. Our church was about five years old at the time, and we had just crossed the 100 barrier, but, as I shared with a close friend, I felt God was about to change some things and we were about to lose some people.

Within a few weeks, I had a stern phone conversation with a woman I had mistakenly given too much freedom and authority to, and things started to unravel. She shared with her large home group that she was leaving, and because she had taken on the role of spiritual mother, they all decided to leave with her.

It would have been hard enough to see all those families leave, but because some of them had other close relationships in the church (as is normal for small churches), by the time the smoke had cleared over the next few months, we had been gutted! Within less than a year, we were down from just over 100 in Sunday attendance to around 50. But it didn't end there. Maybe because it just wasn't a fun place to be anymore or maybe because I had sunk into depression after the wind had been taken out of my sails, some of the more solidly committed also began to find other churches. At the bitter end of the exodus, around a year later, we had settled in at around 25 people—adults and kids. Some of those people are among our closest friends to this day—going through hell together will do that to you.

I had to, once again, find a secular job, and for several weeks, I would sit in my car at lunchtime, crying and begging God to help me grow the church again. But God is never in the same hurry as we are, and He took three more years before things turned around. During those years, God was changing me (remember the prophetic words about a coming change? I should have guessed that most of that changing would be in me!). Those three or four years were the most difficult years of my life. During that time, my wife, Jane, suffered a tubal pregnancy and we lost that baby. Not long afterward, our beloved worship leader's wife died a slow and brutal death from leukemia, which had decided to return after eight years of remission.

Right now you may be thinking, "This is depressing; I should have skipped this chapter," but stay with me, it gets better. One night I came back from a meeting and shared with Jane that I thought God had said it was time to close the church. We cried and cried like we were saying good-bye to someone the doctors had just given up on, and we decided there was nothing left to do but make the "funeral arrangements." But the next day, I felt God was telling me it was not a final death, but more like what happened when Abraham had decided to sacrifice Isaac. I didn't know for sure if I had heard God, but I did know that I didn't have any strength or motivation or an ounce of creativity left in me. I said, "Okay, we'll continue to meet together on Sundays. We'll worship, I'll preach, and we'll go home." And that's exactly what we did. We did nothing else, did nothing differently, but I had emotionally let go of the church. The depressing heaviness I had labored under for the past four years was gone, and all of a sudden people started showing up.

People aren't normally attracted to a church of 25 people, unless it's a new church, which always carries a certain degree of excitement and adventure. But this was not a new church. It was a church that had been in the ICU for the past four years and had nothing new or exciting to offer. But within weeks of that decision to bury the church, there were 40, then 60, then

75 showing up on Sundays. Then we moved into a new facility and continued to grow. Life had returned to what had looked like a corpse, like E.T.'s little red heart vaguely visible through the plastic when everyone thought he was dead.

I now know what it means to see Jesus build His Church. I almost felt like a spectator, as I watched Him bring and enfold people into our little group of motley believers. That experience changed me. I now love the Church. I have discovered that the Church is more than just the sum of its members—it's a living, breathing being that is more precious to Jesus than we can imagine. It has a life of its own; it's His bride!

I've also discovered that in the most barren, hopeless desert of life, the River can change everything and bring new life where there was only defeat, depression, and death. The Holy Spirit, the life-giving River, can transform a barren wasteland into a garden.

Are you in the midst of an impossible situation? Are you a mom or dad whose kid is out of control and on a path of self-destruction? Are you facing a financial nightmare with no end in sight? Have you heard a life-ending prognosis from a respected doctor? Is your marriage on the ropes with no solution on the horizon? Are you a pastor who has grown tired and ready to give up the fight? Then hear this: Our God is a good God and He is firmly in control. He loves you more than you can comprehend! He always cares about His kids, and He always hears when they cry out to Him. He can turn back all the powers of hell mobilized against you, He can turn the desert into a garden, and He can make bananas grow in Alaska!

ENDNOTE

1. Reported in the video "Transformations," by the Sentinel Group.

Chapter 5

SPIRITUAL PHENOMENA

"True revival has commonly been opposed because it came dressed outlandishly, a wild and uncouth invader."
—John White

WHEN WE TALK ABOUT "SPIRITUAL Phenomena," we are simply referring to those curious things that happen in a Holy Spirit-saturated environment, such as people falling to the ground (what is popularly referred to as being "slain in the Spirit"), laughing uncontrollably, trembling, shaking, crying, feeling heat on various parts of their bodies, and a host of other unusual manifestations.

Are these things even worth discussing? Do they really matter? My answer to both of these questions is "No and Yes." "No," because none of these things are what I would call "of first-order importance." That is, they simply are not issues that we should focus on, call attention to, engage in debate over, or lose sleep over. Whether or not any of these things are valid or invalid should not be a front-burner issue for serious bible scholars, theologians, pastors, leaders, or lay-people. None of the things mentioned above necessarily make a person a better disciple, a better person, a better friend, a better husband or wife, or a better church leader.

Having said that, my other answer is "Yes," because they always seem to create a stir, arouse curiosity, bring about confusion or even division, but at the very least call for explanation. Many who have experienced those things testify that they have sensed God's presence in a new and deeper way, or have received new insight or revelation into some important issue in their lives or into scripture, or have felt their faith more grounded than ever. They testify that God now seems more real to them, they love Jesus more than ever, and have a new appreciation for the Person of the Holy Spirit. Often they claim to have a fresh love for God's word and a new motivation to pray or to engage in ministry of some kind.

Whatever your particular bias is toward these spiritual manifestations, they don't seem to be going away, so it's probably helpful to discuss them. I'll tell you up front that my personal bias is to be pretty open to these things, probably because of my early Pentecostal upbringing, but also because I've experienced some of these phenomena enough times to convince me that they are often valid experiences of the Holy Spirit's power. Having said that, the same Pentecostal exposure, along with an M.A. in theology from Fuller Seminary, has made me leery to assume everything done in the name of God is actually from God. Paul was truly inspired by the Holy Spirit, when he wrote, in First Thessalonians 5:19-20, *"Do not put out the Spirit's fire...test everything."* If church leaders can maintain that crucial balance, we may be able to enjoy a long-lasting and healthy revival in the years to come.

At this point, if you lean toward being skeptical of any kind of phenomena like the ones we're discussing, you might say, "I won't put out the Spirit's fire, but I'm not convinced these things are even from the Spirit." And you would have a legitimate concern. To begin with, our starting point in any kind of discussion about spiritual phenomena must be scripture. But be prepared—when we begin to search the bible, we're going to find an abundance of evidence for strange spiritual phenomena, beginning with the ministry of Jesus.

I'm reminded of what a pastor named John Wimber said to some concerned women who confronted him one Sunday, after the Holy Spirit had moved dramatically in his church, Calvary Chapel of Yorba Linda (before it became the Vineyard). They walked up to him and demanded, "Just how far is all of this going to go?" He happened to be carrying his bible, so he held it up and replied, "No farther than this book!" They seemed reassured and left satisfied with his answer. But as John walked away, he thought to himself, "Have they *read* this book? Do they know what's really in here?!"

John knew, as anyone truly familiar with the bible knows, that this book is full of strange things! First, there are the many Old Testament accounts, such as food falling from the sky (manna, in Exodus 16), Elijah stretching himself upon the widow's dead son (II Kings 4), the talking donkey and Balaam talking back to him! (Num. 22), and enough dreams, visions, and miracles to leave conservative church ladies in shock!

There are also dozens of strange phenomena in the New Testament, beginning with the ministry of Jesus. Everyone has heard about Jesus walking on the water and then inviting Peter to do the same (see Matt. 14). On another occasion, when a man who was deaf and could hardly talk was brought to Him, Jesus put His fingers in the man's ears and put spit on the man's tongue (Mark 7)! In the very next chapter, Jesus healed a blind man by spitting on his eyes—how would that go over in your church?!

The book of Acts is filled with accounts of people speaking in tongues or prophesying, along with dramatic healings, miracles, and people being delivered from demons. In chapter 5, Ananias and Sapphira are struck dead for lying. In the same chapter, people brought the sick into the streets so that Peter's shadow might fall on some of them as he passed by, and they were healed! As Stephen was preaching to the Sanhedrin, in Acts 7:55, we are told that *"Stephen, full of the Holy Spirit, looked up to heaven and saw the glory of God and Jesus standing at the right hand of God."* In chapter 8, Philip baptized the eunuch and was immediately transported to another town!

We could list dozens more examples of strange phenomena in the bible and throughout church history, but you get the point: Just because something is strange does not necessarily mean it's not from God. On the other hand, we should not glorify strangeness. Some believers have an unhealthy fascination with strange phenomena, as if the strangeness somehow makes those things more spiritual.

We also need to stress that some of these things are often difficult to explain, because people react differently when acted upon by the Holy Spirit. When someone begins trembling or shaking or falls down in the presence of the Spirit, or feels heat on a part of their body, it is simply their body reacting to the presence of God. The difference in responses from person to person can sometimes be explained in terms of different temperaments, different emotional conditions, theological conditioning, or even crowd dynamics. But we should understand that in almost every revival, when the Holy Spirit comes upon people, strange things (even offensive things) often happen.

I have sometimes thought it would be nice if the Holy Spirit could just move in great power and bring a nation-transforming revival, without any of the messes and controversy that so often seem to accompany revival. But I now believe that is an unrealistic wish, because wherever you have revival, there will always be a degree of messiness. It's never just God. It's always God *in people*.

The late Anglican priest and author, David Watson, told how the Lord helped him understand this. He related how, one afternoon, when he was in his study, the room became stuffy, so he opened a window. A pleasant breeze filled the room, bringing a refreshing change in the air. But suddenly his papers began blowing around and falling all over the floor. Now he had a decision to make: Should he close the window and let the room get stuffy again, so he could have all his papers in order, or should he just leave the window open and find some weights to hold the piles in place? He chose to leave the window open and deal with the breeze the best he could.

That's exactly what it's like when we invite the Holy Spirit. He brings a refreshing breeze that carries with it new life, great joy, a renewal of passion for Jesus, and a wonderful sense of anticipation. But it also creates some complications, unexpected reactions, theological challenges, some discomfort as we give up a measure of control, and even some strange phenomena. The question each of us needs to wrestle with is: How desperate am I for a genuine move of the Holy Spirit? Am I willing to put up with whatever discomfort and controversy comes with the package in order to see true revival? Remember, once you open the window, all bets are off, because the Spirit is the Wind of God, and "the Wind blows wherever it pleases" (see John 3:8).

Now let's take a look at some of these phenomena.

FALLING UNDER THE POWER OF THE SPIRIT (BEING "SLAIN IN THE SPIRIT")

I don't know who came up with the term, "slain in the Spirit," but I've never been comfortable with it. However, the term has gained so much traction over the years that to introduce a new phrase would probably just create confusion, so, for purposes of this book, I've (reluctantly) chosen to stick with it.

My friend John is an engineer and teaches physics at a university nearby. He is highly analytical and skeptical of anything he can't understand. He loves the Lord, but he will not fall down, no matter how many people around him are falling, if he doesn't want to. John shared with me that a few years ago, he and his wife, along with another couple, decided to visit a church in Southern California known for renewal phenomena, because they had heard of the guest speaker. At the end of the message, when the opportunity was given for those wanting prayer, all four of them went forward, along with about 80 other people. Within minutes, his friend was on the floor, then his friend's wife, and then John's wife. But still John stood there. He says he was being blessed as a team prayed for him, but felt no inclination to fall. Even the speaker pointed him out and said, "God's after that guy!" John is not easy to miss—he's about 6'7"—so more people gathered around him to pray, but still John stood. He wasn't trying to be difficult or to "quench the Spirit." He just didn't feel like falling down, so he didn't. I told him that was commendable, because a lot of people would just cave in to peer pressure and fall down, so his "stand" reflected integrity.

But John also related to me another experience years earlier, just weeks after he received Jesus. He had gone with his friends to a church to hear a speaker, and afterward the man came up to John to pray with him for bursitis in his left knee. As John tells it, the guy gently put his hand on his shoulder and began to pray, and before he knew it, he was on the floor, and lay there for some time. When he got up, he felt he had been healed of the bursitis, but was scheduled for surgery the next day. He went to his appointment, but asked the doctor to x-ray the knee, just to be sure, so the doctor consented. Sure enough—no bursitis! John had been healed the night before. Now some might say, "Well, he probably would have been healed even if he didn't end up on the floor." That may be, but at the very least, being "slain in the Spirit" certainly didn't do any harm!

Another man, John Rottman, graduated from Calvin College with majors in Greek and philosophy, earned an MA from the University of St. Michael's College in early Christian history, an MDiv from Calvin Theological Seminary, and a ThD in homiletics from Emmanuel College of the University of Toronto. Prior to his seminary education he worked for five years at a psychiatric hospital in western Michigan. He went on to become a pastor in the Christian Reformed Church and adjunct faculty at Ontario Theological Seminary. Here is his testimony.

> It was not until December in 1995, two days before Christmas, that I went to check out what was happening out at the Airport Vineyard Church. I had always been wary of Pentecostal Christianity, threatened a bit, skeptical too, not supposing it to be something that someone as emotionally stable as myself would find useful or edifying. As a Reformed Christian with a certain amount of curiosity, I did see some value in observing it from afar.
>
> The whole atmosphere that evening rather put me off. I found myself getting increasingly more wary as people around me laughed for no apparent reason, jerked as if in the throes of a mild seizure, or more rarely, staggered up the aisle as if they were drunk.
>
> And yet certain features of the meeting also invited a positive response. The preaching was orthodox, though not spectacular. The offering was underplayed. And both the people who led and those who gave testimonies exuded a kind of unpolished genuineness, an authenticity that was difficult to dismiss as overheated emotionalism or out-and-out charlatanry. They even gave an invitation to accept Jesus Christ at the end of the sermon in classic evangelical style.

As I stood near the front in this sea of people, I couldn't help but notice that many people fell over backwards when people prayed for them. "Well, that is fine for them," I told myself, "but I am not the sort to fall over backwards just to humour some well-intended minister." After a bit of a wait a woman stood in front of me. Since I was dressed in jeans and running shoes, I was a bit startled to have her look at me and confidently say, "I bless upon you the gifts of pastor and teacher." Lucky guess.

She then asked me to extend my hands palms up and to receive what God wanted to give as she prayed. She placed her hands several inches above mine and began to pray that the Holy Spirit would fill me, "like Niagara Falls." I thought this was a bit hokey, but it was her prayer. I further resolved not to play out the fall backwards scenario.

But then several minutes into her prayer, I felt a sort of electric effect like a chill up my spine. And then it was as if someone began to tug firmly at my calf muscles. As my calf muscles involuntarily contracted, I fought falling backwards. And then much to my surprise and embarrassment I found myself lying on my back in front of this strange church. I was fully conscious of the oddness of this event, and also aware of a sort of wave of peace washing over me. And with the peace came a sort of illumination, a sense that everything that I believed about the gospel of Jesus Christ was not mere talk, but really real.

After I had lain there for several moments the woman knelt by me and asked me rather pointedly about a certain aspect of one of my personal relationships. She directed me to pray a prayer of forgiveness, which I did. She went away and after a few minutes I got to my feet and went to look for my friend.

In the days that followed, I found myself spiritually strengthened in several ways. I had never been especially valiant in my prayer life. Prayer was like dieting, if I attended to it with great will power I could maintain a regular prayer life. In the months that followed, I found myself drawn into prayer in new and natural ways. Prayer became more like sailing and less like work. I also found that when I read the Bible, I often had the sense that my attention was being drawn to a particular part of the reading and that it was intended for me at that moment. Could it be God? Further, I found myself strengthened in my fight against an area of temptation in my life that had beset me for many years. I found myself enabled to fight and would describe myself as freed, in that the grip that it held on me was significantly alleviated, though not eliminated.[1]

In Chapter 2, I told the story of Kim, who ended up on the floor after the Holy Spirit came upon her during one of our services. The Lord spoke to her during that "floor time," and she initiated the reconciliation with her mom. Years later, her mother was instantly healed of cancer while at Cedars Sinai Hospital in Los Angeles, and some years after that she received Jesus. All of that wonderful fruit can be traced back to the Holy Spirit working in Kim's life during her time on the floor.

SHAKING, JERKING, WAILING

Here is the witness of Carol Wimber:

On Mother's Day of 1981 we had a watershed experience that launched us into what today is called power evangelism. At this time John [Wimber] invited a young man who had been attending our church to preach on a Sunday evening. By now we had grown to over 700 participants. The young man shared his testimony, which was beautiful and stirring, then asked for all the people under the age of twenty-five to come forward. None of us had a clue as to what was going to happen. When they got to the front the speaker said, "For years now the Holy Spirit has been grieved by the Church, but he's getting over it. Come Holy Spirit."

And He came.

Most of these young people had grown up around our home—we had four children between the ages of fifteen and twenty-one. We knew the young people well. One fellow, Tim, started bouncing. His arms flung out and he fell over, but one of his hands accidentally hit a mic stand and he took it down with him. He was tangled up in the cord, with the mic next to his mouth. Then he began speaking in tongues, so the sound went throughout the gymnasium [where they were meeting]. We had never considered ourselves charismatics, and certainly had never placed emphasis on the gift of tongues. We had seen a few people tremble and fall over before, and we had seen many healings. But this was different. The majority of the young people [over 400] were shaking and falling over. At one point it looked like a battlefield scene, bodies everywhere, people weeping, wailing, speaking in tongues. And Tim in the middle of it all babbling into the microphone. There was much shouting and loud behavior!

John sat by quietly playing the piano and wide-eyed. Members of our staff were fearful and angry. Several people got up and walked out, never to be seen again—at least they were not seen by us.

But I knew that God was visiting us. I was so thrilled, because I had been praying for power for so long. This might not have been the way I wanted to see it come, but this was how God gave it to us...I asked one boy, who was on the floor, "What's happening to you right now?" He said, "It's like electricity. I can't move." I was amazed by the effect of God's power on the human body. I suppose I thought that it would all be an inward work, such as conviction or repentance. I never imagined there would be strong physical manifestations.

But John wasn't as happy as I. He had never seen large numbers of people sprawled out over the floor. He spent that night reading Scripture and historical accounts of revival from the lives of people like Whitefield and Wesley.

...But his study did not yield conclusive answers to questions raised from the previous evening's events. By 5 A.M. John was desperate. He cried out to God, "Lord, if this is you, please tell me." A moment later the phone rang and a pastor friend of ours from Denver, Colorado, was on the line. "John," he said, "I'm sorry I'm calling you so early, but I have something really strange to tell you. I don't know what it means, but God wants me to say, 'It's Me, John.'"[2]

FEELING HEAT

Over many years of ministry experience, I have observed that very often, when individuals are being prayed for (hands-on), they begin to feel heat, either on a specific part of their body, or simply hot all over. When interviewing them later, we have found that there is often a connection between the heat and healing of their bodies. So now, when our team prays for someone, they pause to ask, "What's happening?" If the person indicates that they feel heat, the team is encouraged to keep praying and to ask the Holy Spirit for more power.

There is nothing necessarily spiritual or mystical about the heat. We believe it's simply the body's response to the presence of God. I'm reminded of the time Saul was in pursuit of David in First Samuel 19. When Saul and his men were approaching the place they heard David was supposedly hiding, the Spirit of God came upon them and they prophesied. Saul, however, was so overcome by the presence of God that he stripped off his robes and lay there all day and night. It's very likely that he took off his robes because he was hot.

This story raises another important point: Just because someone experiences some spiritual phenomenon does not mean they are holy or especially pleasing to God. (God had already rejected Saul, and Saul was on a mission to kill David when he became overwhelmed by the Holy Spirit.) It simply means God is present in power. This is good news for most of His children, but could be bad news for those in rebellion!

There have been many books written on the subject of spiritual phenomena. Interestingly, I have hardly ever heard of or read a critic of these phenomena who has experienced any of them. The critics almost consistently are speaking from a lack of experience and from their personal theological bias. What they have sometimes claimed is serious research has been discredited as selective, shoddy, and unscientific when weighed against the facts.[3] But almost universally, those who have had an encounter with the Spirit of God that has resulted in them falling, trembling, shaking, experiencing heat, or other such phenomena, have testified that, indeed, it was God. And their numbers are growing so dramatically that it seems more and more disingenuous to simply dismiss them as "flakes" or their experiences as invalid.

LAUGHTER

In 1994, I traveled to Toronto, because I had heard that God was doing powerful things in one of the local churches, called, at the time, the Airport Vineyard Church. I was not disappointed, as I saw demonstrations of the Spirit's power that surpassed anything I had ever seen before. But the most unusual personal experience happened in a Monday morning prayer meeting with about 20 of us present.

While others were praying various prayers, I began to see a "picture" (the old ship I mentioned in the Introduction), accompanied by a strong impression about what it meant. I stood and shared what I saw with the group, with deep emotion, but as soon as I sat down I felt a powerful eruption of joy coming up from somewhere inside of me. I immediately left for the restroom because I knew what was coming—I had already seen it happen to other people over the last couple of days. As I hurried into the men's room, I came unglued with laughter! I howled and howled as I bounced off the walls, to the point that my stomach hurt. And just when I thought I was composed, here it came again! It felt a little like when I was a kid and my brother had just told me a funny joke during church, and I was doing my best to control my laughter, but all we had to do was look at each other and I would have to cover my mouth and bend over in a futile attempt to stifle my laughter.

I had heard people talking about "holy laughter" before, but I didn't know what to think about it, and for sure had never experienced it until that day in Toronto. But I can tell you now that I did absolutely nothing to bring in on; in fact I tried to exit the scene when it started. I'm a pretty level-headed guy, and people who have known me over the years will tell you that

I've usually leaned toward the analytical/scholarly approach to spiritual things. But as I've reflected on that experience, and the other similar experiences that have followed since then, I've concluded that what God is doing is giving us a little foretaste of the joy that will be ours in the coming kingdom. Now I realize why we're going to need new bodies. The love, peace, and joy God has in store for us simply cannot be contained in these present ones!

MIST AND FIRE

I remember, years ago, hearing Jack Hayford, pastor of Church on the Way in Van Nuys, California, describing the mist that had moved into the sanctuary of his church. He talked about how, when he asked the Lord what it was, the Lord answered that He had chosen the church as a dwelling place for His Spirit.

For the hundreds of thousands who attended the Azusa Street revival in Los Angeles between 1906 and 1910, the visible mist was a common occurrence. For those three and a half years, one of the consistent features, according to eyewitnesses, was the visible presence of God in the form of a heavy mist. In fact, sometimes the mist was so thick that young people actually played hide and seek in it, and babies sleeping under the wooden benches breathed it in. It was in that glorious environment that astounding miracles took place every day for three and a half years.[4]

According to many eyewitness reports, there was also, on several occasions, fire above the building where the Azusa Street services were held. The fire was visible for several blocks, and more than once the fire department showed up, but left after they ascertained there was no danger.[5]

Many students of scripture will immediately remember that smoke and fire also accompanied the presence of God on Mount Sinai, when God met with Moses and gave him the commandments (Exod. 19). Also, at the dedication of Solomon's temple, the presence of God moved into the temple in the form of a cloud, so intense that the priests could not perform their service (I Kings 8:11).

It's interesting to note that William Seymour, the leader of the Azusa Street revival, prophesied that God was going to send an even greater revival in about a hundred years.[6] It appears we may be right on time!

ENDNOTES

1. James Beverly, *Revival Wars* (Ontario, Canada: Evangelical Research Ministries, 1997), 46-48.

2. Carol Wimber in John Wimber and Kevin Springer's book, *Riding the Third Wave* (Basingstoke, Hants: Marshall Pickering, 1987), 45-46, quoted in Don Williams, *Signs, Wonders and the Kingdom of God* (Vine Books, 1989), 89-91.

3. Beverly, *Revival Wars*. One of the better-known critics of the phenomena discussed in this chapter is Hank Hanegraff, author of *Counterfeit Revival*. James Beverly wrote *Revival Wars* partly as a critique of Hanegraff's book. In his introduction, Beverly says he and Hank Hanegraff are friends, and that he encouraged him in his writing of *Counterfeit Revival*. However, he relates his disappointment in Hanegraff's final product: "To my dismay, when I received an advance copy, it was obvious that Hanegraff's work was much inferior to what I would have predicted. I saw immediately that much of his research was outdated and that large portions of his analysis were rooted in faulty logic, selective use of evidence and an inexplicable failure to examine data that was contrary to his own position" (pp. 7-8). Beverly then

goes on to give exhaustive evidence for the next 90 pages.

4. Dr. J. Edward Morris and Cindy McCowan, *They Told Me Their Stories* (Dare to Dream Books, 2010), 21-23, 49-50, 90.

5. Ibid, 37, 101.

6. Ibid, 102.

IT'S NOT ALL GOD!

"Test everything. Hold on to the good."
I Thessalonians 5:21

UP TO THIS POINT, I'VE been talking about things that are dear to my heart and enjoyable to write about—the wind of the Spirit in our sails, the wonderful personality of the Spirit and His effects upon us, and the exciting challenge of doing the works of Jesus, etc. However, this book is not only about the Wind; it's also about the rudder, because no matter how wonderful it is when the wind of the Spirit blows, without a rudder we can easily end up on the rocks of burnout, devastation, or error.

TEST EVERYTHING

If we are committed to maintaining integrity while following the Spirit, it is essential that we learn to discern what is genuinely from God versus what is merely the product of our imaginations or emotions. The ministry of the Spirit is subjective by nature and therefore needs discernment, testing, and confirmation. The fact is, people sometimes make mistakes.

The same scripture that says, *"Do not put out the Spirit's fire; and do not treat prophesies with contempt,"* exhorts us to *"test everything"* (I Thess. 5:19-21). The Holy Spirit is never the problem; the problem arises because the Spirit resides in people!

Some time back, my wife Jane and I had lunch with Rick and Pam Wright, our dear friends, in Pasadena, California. After lunch we walked to the parking lot, and, as they have so effectively done many times, they began to share with us what they felt the Lord had to say to us. But as soon as he sensed his prophetic gift stirring, Rick said, "Hold on a minute," and walked to his car to get his recorder. Rick and Pam had learned to be accountable for every personal prophecy they give by taping themselves and giving a copy to the hearer. This practice not only helps the person receiving the message to have a record to refer back to, but it also protects the person giving the message from being misquoted or misinterpreted.

Two years ago, I traveled to Corona, California, to meet with a man who had ministered deeply to a number of us years earlier. Ken is a pastor, but is also highly gifted prophetically. He and his associate ministered to me through prophecy for more than 30 minutes, while they recorded everything. Then they burned it to a CD and gave it to me. Over the past two years, my wife and I have listened to that CD many times, and continue to be encouraged and blessed by those wonderful words given by the Spirit. It has also given us the safety of being able to test that message over time.

THE RUDDER OF THE CHURCH

Unlike the Old Testament, when there were only one or two prophets for the nation, in the New Testament gifts such as prophecy have been dispersed broadly to the Church, and we each only get a part of the package. God has purposely designed it that way, so that we would depend on each other for the full expression of His revelations. It was Paul, who, in

First Corinthians 13, said, *"we prophesy in part..."* Then he went on in chapter 14 to emphasize the fact that every member of the Body needs every other member. It takes all of the parts to complete the picture.

The concept of the lone ranger is unbiblical. In Hebrews 10:25, for example, the author strongly exhorts us to not give up on meeting together with other believers, but to keep encouraging one another. It is one of many "one-another" scriptures, which emphasize the importance of maintaining healthy relationships with a group of Christians. Prophecy, along with all of the other gifts of the Spirit, is highly desirable, but should be tested, so stay connected!

After I had my dramatic encounter with God at Mission Valley Church in Fremont, California, in the summer of 1971, I set off for bible college in Oklahoma City. I was "on fire" with passion for God, but I also realized the need for preparation before embarking on serious ministry. I was doing well and enjoying my classes, but about halfway into the first quarter we had a guest speaker who fanned my flames for evangelism. I decided to quit school and go back to California to get on with the "real business" of "winning souls." I shared my heartfelt passion with some of my friends and two of my teachers, who all felt I was making a mistake. On their advice, I decided to give it a few days, and, after the initial euphoria faded, I decided I still had a few things to learn!

There is great value in getting confirmation of our impressions from other mature believers. Proverbs 11:14 says, *"...in the abundance of counselors there is victory"* (NASB). I know of far too many believers who thought God was leading them in a direction and took action based on their own impressions without going to more mature believers or church leaders for their input, and they ended up making costly mistakes.

One of the most valuable resources we have for providing stability and health as we pursue the exciting but subjective world of the Spirit is the Body of Christ. This becomes especially important when developing spiritual gifts, such as prophecy, or when learning to interpret dreams, visions, inner impressions, etc. It is when individuals function without accountability, or are not grounded in healthy fellowship with a group of Christians, that they become "loose cannons," and vulnerable to erroneous guidance.

We experienced this firsthand a few years ago, when considering an expansion of our facility. We lease space in a large commercial building, and when a major tenant moved out next door, I did a walk-through of their space. I could immediately see how this move could benefit our church, and I felt God was leading us to expand, but there was the matter of finances (not an uncommon issue for churches leasing commercial space in California). I found out what the build-out for the new auditorium would cost and arranged a meeting of our leadership team in the new space. After giving them the tour, we sat down in one of the rooms and decided to commit the matter to God in prayer. We had been learning about "listening prayer," and after our prayer time one of the ladies said, "I keep getting the word, 'wait.'" This was not the word I wanted to hear, and she could tell. She went on to say, "I'm not saying the Lord means to wait a long time; it could just be a week or two. I don't know, I just keep hearing 'wait.'" Several of the others agreed, so we talked about how to proceed.

There was another party who had approached the building owner about the facility, so naturally I felt a little nervous and impatient; I didn't want this opportunity to be snatched out from under us. But we did feel that we needed to trust God in the matter, so we decided to wait at least a week or two before making a firm decision, and in the meantime we would let the church know about the opportunity. This would allow us more time to sift through our impressions, weigh pros and cons, and to see if the finances would be there, at least to a large enough degree to make us comfortable moving forward.

The following Sunday, right after worship, I shared the matter with the congregation and we adjourned to the vacant area for a tour. We had labeled the rooms and offices and explained how the new auditorium would be configured. Then we simply asked them to pray and ask God how much they should give toward this project, and told them we would receive an offering the following Sunday.

The following Friday, two days before the Sunday we were to receive the offering, my wife and I had an appointment with a woman in our church. She had been through a divorce before coming to our church, and two years prior her teenage son had been killed in a freak pole-vaulting accident at school. By this time she had decided it was time to get on with her life, and we assumed she just wanted us to counsel her regarding a new relationship she had been considering.

Shortly after we all sat down in the restaurant, she began sharing with us the bittersweet news that her ex-husband had just won a legal settlement over the fatal accident and that she wanted to tithe on her share. She asked that part of the money be used to set up a memorial fund for the youth group, in her son's name, but said that we could use the rest in any way we saw fit. This part alone came to most of the amount required for the build-out we were contemplating!

My wife and I were aghast, but tried to subdue our excitement. I said to her, "This is amazing timing! You know about the build-out project we've asked the church to pray about, right?" She said, "No, what project?" She hadn't been at church the previous Sunday and didn't even know about the whole expansion we had been considering, but God had arranged everything to coincide perfectly! Armed with this great news, the leaders now felt excited about moving forward, and I was so glad I had followed their advice to wait. When we submit our impressions to other mature believers, things almost always work out better.

I could talk about many other instances where I thought God had spoken to me, some of which turned out to be just my own thoughts or desires, or others that were confirmed later to indeed have been from God. But in all cases where I turned to a group of mature Christians for confirmation and further guidance, God blessed my actions and protected me from decisions that would have been counterproductive. As Proverbs 11:14 says, *"In the multitude of counselors there is wisdom"* (AMP).

In Acts 13:1-3, a group of leaders in the church gathered together for a time of fasting and prayer, during which the Holy Spirit gave specific instructions about sending Paul (then called "Saul") and Barnabas on their first mission. We are not told how this message came, but most likely through a message of prophecy by one of them. Even then, they continued fasting and praying (probably to establish with certainty that it really was the Lord who had spoken), after which Paul and Barnabas were commissioned. In their minds, there was no doubt that this prophetic "word" was from God. Luke writes, *"The two of them, sent on their way **by the Holy Spirit**..."* (emphasis mine). Here is modeled for us, superbly, the value and strength of the church community when we are attempting to hear from God.

These examples show how important it is for individuals seeking to follow the Spirit not to become independent, but to be well-grounded in relationship with a group of mature Christians. But it is equally important for entire churches, and even church movements, to maintain a sense of community and partnership with the larger Body of Christ. When we only read the books or magazines of our denomination or movement, when we only attend their conferences and seminars, and listen only to their speakers, we rob ourselves of a great wealth of wisdom and strength the Holy Spirit has deposited in other parts of the church.

I have discovered great value in the diversity of gifts and teachings scattered throughout the larger Church, and I believe I am a better man for having been influenced by many brothers and sisters from traditions different from my own. Without the variety of these truths being spoken into our lives, I believe we run the risk of denominational error and elitism. The Bride of Christ is beautiful in her entirety! Let's not limit the command to "love one another" to only those of our particular tribe.

THE RUDDER OF SCRIPTURE

The most important piece of the "rudder" that will keep us headed in the right direction as we pursue a Spirit-empowered life is a high view of scripture. A good knowledge of God's word is the very foundation for life and ministry. In our passionate desire to hear God's voice, we need to be reminded that God has already spoken abundantly over centuries through His prophets, His apostles, and His Son, and that these profoundly powerful truths have been written down for our benefit. Any contemporary prophecies or "words" from God have to first be consistent with God's previous prophecies, teachings, or revelations in scripture. Very simply, God will not contradict Himself.

Some of my most memorable times of God's dealings with me personally, and many of my most powerful revelations from the Holy Spirit, have come during those intimate times of prayerful reflection on God's word. The same was true of men like John Wesley, Charles Finney, Jonathan Edwards, the Apostle Paul, and others—men who lived and ministered in the Spirit's power. The written word of God is our most valuable resource and a treasure-filled storehouse of knowledge, wisdom, and power. It is the book of the Spirit, and its pages are filled with life. As we pursue the Spirit-empowered life, let's make sure we simultaneously develop a heart hungry for

God's word. The Author loves His book and is honored and pleased when we do also.

In Second Timothy 2:15, Paul exhorted Timothy to make every effort to correctly understand and teach the word. Time, effort, and diligence are required to properly interpret the ancient scriptures, but it is a discipline that is rewarded richly. Proverbs 25:2 says, *"It is the glory of God to conceal a matter; to search out a matter is the glory of kings."* Many of God's greatest treasures in scripture are "hidden," in a sense, and require a seeking and determined heart to uncover. But we are told that this noble search is a kingly pursuit and that our efforts will certainly be rewarded.

During the Jesus Movement in the 1970's, I was attending Fuller Seminary in Pasadena, California. One Friday night, I decided to drive down to a church service at Calvary Chapel, Costa Mesa, which was the hub of the Jesus Movement in Southern California at the time. I was amazed at what I found.

I had heard and read many reports about the youth revival that was sweeping California and about thousands being baptized in the ocean and being set free from drugs and self-destructive lifestyles. What I hadn't counted on were the crowds of long-haired young people swarming into the church carrying well-worn bibles. In my years as a pastor's kid and then as a pastor, I was not used to seeing so many bibles in such terrible shape! These people were obviously serious about reading the bible. I have discovered since then, that many of the historic revivals, including those documented as far back as the Old Testament, included a renewed hunger for God's written word.

Very often, revivals of individual people also begin with a growing desire for God's word, and these personal revivals are continually fueled by the word. When God began drawing me back to Himself in 1971, after a four-year period of rebellion, one of the first signs that something was changing was that I suddenly found myself being drawn to the bible. Then, after my great encounter with God that summer, I began taking my paperback "Good News for Modern Man" version of the bible to work, and I looked forward every day to lunchtime, not only for the break, but mostly because I would be able to read my bible. The Spirit was at work in me, and He was driving me to His word.

Nicky Gumbel, founder of the famous Alpha course, relates how a similar thing happened to him at the beginning of his own spiritual pilgrimage. He was a law student and had a very skeptical mind, but had become curious about the Christian faith. Someone had suggested that he try reading the bible, so he went home that night and read through all four gospels. The next day he picked up where he'd left off and kept reading... Acts, Romans, both books of Corinthians, Galatians, Ephesians...then the following day continued reading until he had finished reading the entire New Testament! At the end of his reading, he exclaimed, "It's all true!" The Spirit had done His work through His word.

One of the things we can expect to see as the Holy Spirit stirs anew in the Western world is a renewed passion for the bible, especially among young people. And this is something we ought to be proactively praying for, because not only is hunger for the bible a sign of the Spirit's presence, but it can provide both the spark and the fuel for a healthy and sustained spiritual awakening.

Chapter 7

Spiritual Tools

*"Now about spiritual gifts, brothers, I do not want
you to be ignorant."* I Corinthians 12:1

THE THREE PRIMARY CHAPTERS IN the New Testament that talk about gifts God has given to the church are Romans 12, First Corinthians 12, and Ephesians 4. My understanding is that these three passages describe three categories of gifts that are distinct in nature from each other. I will attempt to give a summary of these passages and what I believe God's intent was in each of them, but my main focus in this chapter is on the gifts listed in First Corinthians 12:8-10, because it is those gifts that are attributed specifically to the Holy Spirit. As I do this, I realize that there may be disagreement from some who have a different understanding of spiritual gifts, but, again, the intent of this chapter is not to give a comprehensive discussion of all of the gifts God has given. That would take volumes, and there are many books written on the subject by authors of different theological persuasions.

I am choosing to focus on the gifts in First Corinthians 12:8-10 for the following reasons: (1) It is my conviction that these gifts are available to every believer in Christ (unlike many of the gifts discussed in the other passages, such as apostle, pastor, administrator, etc.), yet it is equally clear to me that these powerful gifts, or "tools" are vastly underutilized. (2) Most people have little difficulty in understanding the designations of "pastor," "evangelist," "leadership," "administration," "giving," or "serving," for example, but there is a great lack of understanding of the gifts listed in the First Corinthians 12 passage we will be discussing. (3) Understanding these Spirit-given tools can vastly increase your effectiveness as a servant of Christ.

In Romans 12:6-8, Paul discusses gifts such as prophesying, serving, teaching, encouraging, giving, leadership, governing, and showing mercy. His emphasis in this passage is on humility and mutual appreciation, while valuing the different functions of each member.[1] These are identifiable characteristics that enable various individuals to exercise different *functions* in the church. They are not spontaneous endowments for specific occasions, but rather characteristics or "vested" qualities that people can identify as "traits."

In Ephesians 4:11-12, Paul says, *"It was He* [Jesus] *who gave some to be apostles, some to be prophets, some to be evangelists, and some to be pastors and teachers, to prepare God's people for works of service, so that the body of Christ may be built up…."* Here it is clear that Jesus has appointed these individuals for the purpose of equipping the church for service. In the verses that follow, Paul goes on to show that when this is working the way God has intended, the church will experience long-term growth and health. This passage describes Jesus' "gifts" to the church as people who hold established "offices" through which to minister strength and health to the body of Christ. Again, as in the passage in Romans 12, these "gifts" are permanent in nature, and become identified with the individuals.

When he introduces the passage in First Corinthians 12:8-10, however, Paul uses the Greek word, *phanerosis*, which is interpreted, "manifestations" in verse 7. The gifts that follow are "manifestations" or "demonstrations" of the Spirit's activity. This is important to understand, because, as such, these "gifts" are given by the Spirit, who moves "just as He determines" (verse 11) for any specific occasion. This sounds remarkably like what Jesus said about the work of the Spirit in John 3:8: *"The wind blows wherever it pleases...so it is with everyone born of the Spirit."*

These are not vested or permanent gifts like the gifts in the other "gift" passages, but are given at the moment they are needed to whomever is available and chosen by the Spirit for that specific occasion. They can, however, be developed and nurtured for greater effectiveness, as the repetition of these endowments occurs, and as our experience grows.

In fact, some individuals become so effective in specific gifts of the Spirit, such as prophecy, that they develop what many call a "ministry of prophecy." Even then, it is my opinion that they still do not necessarily hold the "office" of prophet. For example, I know several pastors who function quite effectively and consistently in the gift of prophecy, but they are still pastors, and not prophets.[2]

Several more observations need to be made before we examine each of the gifts or "tools" of the Spirit:

First, there are those who believe that the nine gifts listed here are not the complete list, and that Paul was simply rattling off some examples. While I am open to that possibility, I have not heard of other gifts of the Spirit that fit the context of this passage to my satisfaction. However, as I said, I remain open to that possibility and welcome further discussion.

Second, Paul has made it clear that these gifts have great value for every believer. Not only does he say, in First Corinthians 12:1, that he does not want us to be "ignorant" concerning these gifts; he says in both First Corinthians 12:31 and First Corinthians 14:1 that we should "eagerly desire" these gifts.

This makes even more sense if Jesus is, in fact, our model for ministry, since He demonstrated these gifts so effectively. Each one of us should ask ourselves, "Am I truly eager for the gifts of the Holy Spirit?"

Third, the impact of the gifts of the Spirit is so much greater when cloaked in love. Jesus modeled for us the effectiveness of power combined with love, compassion, and grace. We discuss this more in Chapter 8, "The Treasure in the Middle."

Fourth, these are "grace gifts." That means the Spirit does not give these gifts only to those who are "deserving" or "mature." A person who has just received Jesus is able, potentially, to exercise spiritual gifts, and so is anyone who still has obvious character flaws. Our parents did not give us presents at Christmas or on our birthdays because we had done everything right the past year, but because of their goodness and generosity. How much more true is this of God! This means we should not be too quickly impressed with those who minister powerfully through the gifts of the Spirit. It's not necessarily because of their godliness, but His grace. Only time will tell whether they have admirable character undergirding their gifting.

Years ago, in one of the *Dennis the Menace* episodes, Dennis and his friend Joey went to visit Mr. Wilson, their neighbor, who kindly gave them some cookies. When they had left the house, Joey said to Dennis, "Gee, Dennis, we must have done something really special for Mr. Wilson to give us cookies." "Oh no," Dennis replied, "Mr. Wilson doesn't give us cookies because *we're* nice; he gives us cookies because *he's* nice!" In the same way, God doesn't necessarily give us gifts because we deserve them, but because of His grace and kindness.

Fifth, many believers have already experienced spiritual gifts without knowing it. As we discuss gifts, such as the "word of knowledge" or "discerning of spirits," for example, you may recognize that God has given you these gifts on past occasions. Hopefully, armed with some language and more understanding, you will find yourself increasing in faith and able to nurture these gifts to greater effectiveness.

Finally, there is disagreement about the labels attached to these gifts. For example, some, like theologian Gordon Fee, whom I greatly respect, maintain that what many Pentecostals and Charismatics call a "word of knowledge," actually would fall under the heading of "prophecy." However, I have chosen, for ease of communication, to use the terms that are most commonly employed when referring to these gifts.

A thorough and comprehensive discussion of each of these endowments of the Spirit would require a whole book in itself, and, helpful as that may be, that is not my purpose for this book. So, what follows in this chapter is a sort of compromise between a brief summary and an extensive teaching. There have been many attempts to categorize this list of gifts, but I'm simply going to go through them in the order they appear in scripture. Here goes:

THE WORD OF WISDOM
(GREEK: *LOGOS SOPHIAS*)

A Word of Wisdom is an utterance inspired by God and spoken by an individual. It is "seeing" what God "sees" and applying God's wisdom to a specific situation.

We have already discussed some examples of this gift in previous chapters. For example, in Chapter 1, I related the story of how God impressed me to take the family for ice cream, which broke the tension that had filled our home. Also, in Chapter 3, under the section, "Learning to Hear," I shared our experience in Uganda when God gave Mike Flynn an impression that we were not to have the car serviced, but to press on, and that everything would be okay.

Jesus exercised this gift on many occasions. For example, in Mark 12:13-17, when the Pharisees and Herodians tried to trap Jesus, it says, *"They came to Him and said, 'Teacher...is it right to pay taxes to Caesar or not?'"* This was an obvious no-win situation, in which, regardless of how He answered, it seemed He would be in trouble with someone. If He said they should pay taxes, the people would turn against Him; and if He said they should not, the authorities could have Him arrested. But Jesus simply said, *"Bring me a denarius,"* and asked, *"Whose portrait is this? And whose inscription?"* To which they replied, "Caesar's." Then Jesus said to them, *"Give to Caesar what is Caesar's and to God what is God's."*

In Genesis 41, God gave Joseph not only the interpretation of Pharaoh's dreams, but the wisdom to know what course of action to take. When Joseph had interpreted the dream about the coming economic prosperity and subsequent meltdown, he went on to advise Pharaoh about storing one-fifth of the prosperous harvest to provide for the lean times to follow. This message of wisdom so impressed Pharaoh and his officials, that Joseph was made the most powerful ruler in all of Egypt, second only to Pharaoh. The Spirit still gives messages of wisdom today. Maybe God wants to use you as He did Joseph!

A friend of mine has done very well buying, developing, and selling real estate in California. A few years ago he had a dream in which he saw a long caravan of camels carrying many goods. The line of camels was so long he couldn't see the end. After he and his wife prayed about the meaning of the dream, they felt God was telling them there was a long season of economic prosperity beginning. He immediately began buying all the real estate he and his partners could handle, developing and flipping some properties, holding on to others.

Several years later he had another dream. This time he saw a similar caravan of camels, only this time he could see the end. He realized God was showing him the season of prosperity in the real estate market was about to end, so he and his partners began selling everything, making handsome profits on every deal. Sure enough, not long after, the bull market ended for real estate in Southern California, but God had rescued him and prospered him in advance of it! (Incidentally, I happen to know that this friend of mine is faithful in tithes and offerings, and has a truly generous heart. No wonder God can trust him with wealth!)

THE WORD OF KNOWLEDGE
(*LOGOS GNOSEOS*)

In this gift, the Spirit imparts information that He wants shared, to a person or group, on a specific occasion.

In my own experience, this gift has had a profound impact as a catalyst for spiritual breakthrough, as I shared in Chapter 2, regarding my dramatic encounter by the Spirit at the age of twenty-one.

There are several examples of this gift having similarly profound impacts upon people in the New Testament. In the account of Jesus talking with the Samaritan woman in John 4, at one point in the conversation Jesus said to her, *"Go, call your husband and come back." "I have no husband," she replied. Jesus said to her, "You are right when you say you have no husband. The fact is, you have had five husbands, and the man you now have is not your husband...."* The story continues with her being so powerfully impacted by this that she goes back to her village, effusively telling people, *"Come, see a man who told me everything I ever did!"* The villagers then meet Jesus for themselves and beg Him to stay with them. John records that Jesus did stay for two days, with the result that many more became believers!

Earlier in the first chapter of John's gospel, we are told that Philip found Nathanael and brought him to Jesus. John says, *"When Jesus saw Nathanael approaching, He said of him, 'Here is a*

true Israelite, in whom there is nothing false.' 'How do You know me?'
Nathanael asked. Jesus answered, 'I saw you while you were still under
the fig tree before Philip called you.' Then Nathanael declared, 'Rabbi,
You are the Son of God; You are the King of Israel!'" What a dramatic response for a first introduction to Jesus! And all because
the Spirit gave Jesus a Word of Knowledge for Nathanael.

This gift has the potential to impact people in such profound
ways that we have made it our practice to give opportunity for
people to share this gift during many of our Sunday services.
However, I believe that this gift has even greater potential outside of our church settings. Just as Jesus was used by the Spirit
to exercise this gift for the purpose of evangelizing a Samaritan village, so He wants to use us to reach our communities for
Christ. (Some people who are leading the way in "prophetic
evangelism" are Doug Addison and Robby Dawkins in the
U.S., and Mark Stibbe in the U.K.)

THE GIFT OF FAITH (*PISTIS*)

There are several different kinds of faith. For example,
there is the faith that a people exercise when they trust Jesus
as savior; there is the kind of faith that helps you believe God
will do what He has promised (the opposite of unbelief); and
there is your life as a believer in Jesus, sometimes referred to
as "the Christian faith." But the *gift* of faith is different. It has a
supernatural flavor and often has remarkable results.

James Dunn's definition of this gift goes like this: "[The Gift
of] Faith is the mysterious surge of confidence which sometimes arises within a person faced with a specific situation or
need. It gives that person a trans-rational certainty and assurance that God is about to act through a word or action."[3]

Years ago, when Jane and I were living in Oklahoma City,
we received a distressing phone call that her father would
have to undergo emergency surgery for a seriously ulcerated

stomach. The problem was that he had had heart surgery not too long before that, so naturally the doctors were concerned that his heart might not be able to endure the procedure.

Having received this news, Jane and I knelt down at the sofa in our living room and began to pray. Within a few minutes, a sense of peace came over us, and we felt assured that everything was going to work out, and that her father would be okay. Later that day her mother called to say that the surgery went ahead as scheduled, but when the doctors began to explore her father's stomach, they could find no trace of ulcers—only a clean and healthy stomach! God had given us a gift of faith, which produced the assurance that there would be a positive outcome.

In First Kings 18, we find the amazing story of Elijah challenging the prophets of Baal to a showdown. After they spent the day crying out to their god to no avail, Elijah took over. He built an altar to the God of Israel, and then commanded that water be poured over the altar and the sacrifice. He was so certain that God was going to answer by fire, that he ordered more and more water to be poured over the altar, to the point that it even overflowed the trench around the altar. Then he prayed a simple prayer, and God sent the fire! God had given Elijah a gift of faith, and nothing could shake it.

There are many other examples of this gift in both Old and New Testaments, especially in the ministry of Jesus and in Acts. Often it overlapped with gifts of healings or miracles, but occasionally even came into play in judgment. For example, in Acts 5:9-10, Peter pronounced death upon Sapphira, and she immediately fell down dead; or Acts 13:11, when Paul declared that Elymas would be blind for a season, and he immediately was struck with blindness. But most often this gift is used in conjunction with healings, such as when Jesus pronounced someone healed, even long distance, as in Matthew 8:13, when Jesus pronounced the centurion's servant healed, or Matthew

15:28, when Jesus told the woman her daughter had been delivered. Peter and John were given this gift in Acts 3:1-7, when they healed the crippled man at the gate of the temple.

According to Jesus, faith is an extraordinarily valuable commodity. Each of us would benefit tremendously, and would be of great help to the world, by prayerfully pursuing this gift. In the process, we will likely need to repent of those pockets of unbelief that afflict so many of us.

GIFTS OF HEALING (LITERALLY "GIFTS OF HEALINGS"; GREEK: *CHARISMATA IAMATON*)[4]

If we accept that Jesus' ministry was the template for our ministries, then perhaps this gift stands out above the others listed in First Corinthians 12, with the possible exception of prophecy. More than any other gift, Jesus' ministry was characterized by the healing of sick people, and this gift frequently overlapped with faith and the working of miracles.

A few Sundays ago, I asked how many had personally experienced a "divine" healing or miracle. I was amazed that fully a third of the people in our church claimed to have been healed directly by God, apart from the intervention of doctors. In this arena of healing, I believe we need to have a holistic understanding of the way God works.

Most of us have benefited enormously from the medical profession. (My own daughter is currently in medical school, so before long we will have a doctor in our own family.) There is absolutely no reason to discourage people from seeking medical treatment when they need it. But neither is there any reason to discourage people from asking God to heal them directly. Someone has joked that the difference between Baptists and Pentecostals is that Baptists, when they get sick, see the doctor first, and if that doesn't help, they pray; Pentecostals, on the other hand, when they get sick, pray first, and if that doesn't work, they go to the doctor!

Whatever our theological or ecclesiastical background, healing is a subject that the Church at large needs to become immersed in, and to master. There are few things that result in more glory to God, more help to people, and have greater evangelistic potential than experiencing God's healing touch! By God's grace, we need to work through and lay aside any hesitancy or ambivalence in the area of healing. One needs to look no farther than the ministry of Jesus to see how important this gift is.

The practice of healing the sick is founded upon the conviction that God is a loving, compassionate, and merciful God. Jesus has demonstrated God's will so consistently and powerfully in this area that there should be no doubt in our minds that God wants people well. Any theology which denies that God heals people today is simply a false theology. It cannot stand up under an unbiased examination of scripture; it cannot stand up under the testimony of history; and it cannot stand up under the testimony of countless thousands today who have personally experienced healing.

In His conversation with the Canaanite woman (Matt. 15:21-28; Mark 7:24-30), Jesus made it clear that healing is the children's "bread." Just as bread was the staple food of that time, healing is not a special grace, reserved for special or "spiritual" or holy people; it is the very staple of our lives—the gracious provision of a generous God! In Exodus 15:26, God revealed Himself as "The God who heals," and Matthew 8:17 testifies that, in healing the sick, Jesus fulfilled the prophecy of Isaiah, that *"He took up our infirmities and carried our diseases."* Then, according to First Corinthians 12:9, the Spirit gives this gift to the body of Christ. Notice from these passages: Father, Son, and Holy Spirit—the entire Trinity—are committed to healing people. My strong conviction is that God's healing is meant to extend to our entire being—physical, spiritual, relational, and emotional.

How do you exercise this gift? First, by simply asking. In First Corinthians 14, Paul exhorts us to eagerly desire the gifts that most benefit the Church. And Jesus promised that if we ask, we will receive; if we seek, we will find; and if we knock, the door will be opened. (The Greek tenses of these verbs all imply continuous, persistent action, as in "keep asking, keep seeking, keep knocking.") Second, just begin praying for everyone you come in contact with who needs to be healed. We grow in effectiveness as we exercise this gift, just like with every gift. Offering to pray for people always involves a measure of risk, but "faith is spelled R-I-S-K!"[5] Third, learn from others who have more experience than you. The fact is, some prayers are more effective (and more scripturally sound) than others.[6]

WORKING OF MIRACLES
(*ENERGEMATA DUNAMEON*)

Miracles are events in which people and things are beneficially affected by an extraordinary power of God working through an individual. This gift, perhaps more than the others, can intimidate even the most mature follower of Jesus. We can imagine ourselves laying hands on someone and seeing God heal their headache, or gathering with a group of elders and anointing a sick person with oil and watching as they quickly become well, but to be part of a true miracle is a real stretch of our faith. However, I am confident that as we understand the biblical context of miracles, we will come to believe that this gift belongs to the Church just as much as any of the other gifts.

Webster's Dictionary defines a miracle as "An extraordinary event manifesting divine intervention in human affairs, or as an extremely outstanding or unusual event, thing, or accomplishment."

The New Testament frequently uses the words "signs" and "wonders" to refer to miracles. They were "signs," in that they authenticated the message of Jesus, and, later, the message of His followers. They were "wonders," because they aroused in people a sense of awe and wonder at the power of God and the message about Jesus. So miracles can have a purpose beyond themselves: To point people to Jesus Christ.

Before we go on, and just to keep things in perspective, let me emphasize that the greatest miracle happens when someone is born again through faith in Jesus Christ. Just as a new baby is truly a miracle—a perfect human being appearing from what began as a microscopic marriage between a sperm and an egg—so every time a person is born spiritually, a miracle happens! This means that when you or I help someone find Jesus, we get to participate in the greatest miracle!

Miracles are powerful testimonies to the truth about Jesus and the goodness of God, and tend to proliferate where evangelism is happening among unreached people groups, in the power of the Spirit. Heidi Baker, who has worked for years among the AIDS orphans of Zimbabwe, says that in addition to personally witnessing dozens instantly healed of blindness and other diseases, she claims to have seen over a hundred people raised from the dead![7] These miracles, and her extraordinary love for the people of Africa, help explain how she and her husband, Roland, have helped to plant over 7,000 churches throughout Africa.

Many instances of healing would fall into the category of miracles, such as when Jesus healed the blind, deaf, or crippled. However, they would also include things like turning water into wine and walking on water. Of course, among the greatest miracles in the bible would have to be the conception of Jesus by the Holy Spirit in the Virgin Mary, the raising of Lazarus from death after four days, and the resurrection of Jesus.

Our great challenge today is to believe that what Jesus said in John 14:12 applies to all believers, and that we should aggressively pursue a ministry that includes miracles. In that passage, Jesus said, *"I tell you the truth, anyone who has faith in Me will do what I have been doing. He will do even greater things than these, because I am going to the Father."* As mind-blowing as that statement seems, we must understand that Jesus was challenging His followers, as He consistently did, to embrace the pursuit of what seems impossible to man, because, *"what is impossible with man is possible with God"* (Luke 18:27).

There is, today, a growing list of eminent theologians, who emphatically maintain that the promise of Jesus in John 14:12 applies to all believers, and that He was specifically talking about performing miracles. For example, in referring to this passage, Professor C.H. Dodd of Cambridge "points out that the 'works' in question are the miraculous works of Christ."[8]

Gary Greig and Kevin Springer, in their book, *The Kingdom and the Power*, point out that "the plain grammatical and lexical meaning of the passage and related passages in the Gospel of John all show that the 'greater works' are primarily the miraculous works of Jesus, which He promises to work through anyone who believes in Him."[9]

In addition to actual miracles, there are also many times when God intervenes in our lives in ways that are truly miraculous. For example, my wife Jane's parents were missionaries to Cuba in the late 1950's, when Castro came to power. Their mail was routinely opened, and many times money had been stolen out of the envelopes by the time they got the letters. On one occasion, they had run out of money and had no more food in the house. After her parents had put the three little girls to bed, they knelt down and prayed together that God would provide food for their family. Early the next morning, there was a knock on the door, and a Cuban man stood there, looking a little sheepish. He explained that he had a grocery store down the street, that he felt he was to help them, and that they were welcome to come and get whatever they needed. By the time the girls woke up, breakfast was ready, same as always, and they didn't know that this breakfast had been a miracle until years later.

What's so remarkable about this story is the fact that most Cubans, at that time, assumed all Americans were rich, and yet this stranger had been moved upon by God, in answer to prayer, to offer groceries to this American family!

For the church in Galatia, it was apparently quite normal to experience miracles in their midst. In Galatians 3:5, Paul makes a seemingly off-hand remark about this when he wrote to them, *"Does God give you the Spirit and work miracles among you because you observe the law, or because you believe what you have heard?"* His point was that their (normal) experience of miracles and other signs of the Spirit was not because of their adherence to the law, but because of their faith in Jesus. How about us? Do we believe that God still wants to work miracles in our church? Do we believe that "Jesus Christ is the same, yesterday, today and forever" (Heb. 13:8)?

PROPHECY (*PROPHETEIA*)

James Dunn says, "Prophecy is declaring the message of God to his Church for the purpose of edification. It is not a skill, aptitude or talent. It is the actual speaking forth of words given by the Spirit in a particular situation and ceases when the words (given by the Spirit) cease.[10]

The gift of prophecy is the greatest of all of the gifts of the Spirit. That's because God's spoken word has enormous power to change lives, situations, churches, and even nations. Of all gifts, prophecy is the one mentioned the most in the New Testament. According to Paul, in First Corinthians 14:3, *"…everyone who prophesies speaks to men for their strengthening, encouragement and comfort."*

In Second Chronicles chapter 20, King Jehoshaphat had just been told that a vast army was marching on Judah. Alarmed, he called for a fast and had the nation gather with him to seek God's help. After he led the crowd in prayer, the Spirit of the Lord came upon Jahaziel, who prophesied that Jehoshaphat was not to be afraid, but was to march out to meet the enemy. He even gave the king the exact time and place where they would find the enemy! Then he told him that they would not even have to fight, because the battle was not theirs, but the Lord's.

This word from the Lord had such a powerful impact on King Jehoshaphat and the people that they set out the next morning, with the choir out in front of the army, singing praises to God! The king and all the people of Judah went from being filled with fear and anxiety one minute, to being filled with faith, joy, and confidence the next. This is the power of prophecy. By the time they arrived at the location that had been prophesied, the entire enemy army lay dead, and all they had to do was to gather the spoils!

Many stories, in both the Old and New Testaments, testify to the power of prophecy, and the early church experienced the blessing of prophecy as a normal part of their corporate life. But we need to embrace this gift for ourselves and for our churches today. I have personally received great encouragement, comfort, and direction from this gift.

My associate, Mike Flynn, shared with me recently how personal prophetic messages have benefited him. On one of these occasions, while he was attending a conference in Boulder, Colorado, at which Dick Mills was speaking, Mike and his wife, Sue, decided to go to an Olive Garden restaurant for lunch. While they were eating, Dick and his wife walked in and immediately went over to Mike. Dick pointed at Mike and said to him, "This is an unusual word, but God's word for you is 'mahanaim.'" Now this word first appears in Genesis 32:2, and means "two camps."

Mike had been a priest in the Episcopal Church for years, but had recently discovered the Vineyard movement and had been drawn to its founder, John Wimber.

That word from Dick Mills has provided great comfort to Mike over the years since then, as he has wrestled over his relationship to the Episcopal Church. To this day, Mike successfully conducts healing seminars and conferences in both of these "camps."

DISTINGUISHING BETWEEN SPIRITS OR DISCERNMENT OF SPIRITS (*DIAKRISEIS PNEUMATON*)

This gift enables the person to know whether the source operating through a person is demonic, divine, or simply human. It has sometimes been called, "The police gift," because it exposes evil and leads to its arrest.

Note that this is not called, simply, the gift of discernment. Discernment, as the term is normally used, refers to the ability to make good judgments about specific situations or people, which comes to us as we mature as disciples of Jesus. But the gift of discerning of spirits refers specifically to the ability to determine whether there is demonic activity present, or whether it is the Holy Spirit working, or whether there is simply a human dysfunction or character issue surfacing. It should also be noted that very often emotional illness can seem a lot like demonization, which is why one should be very slow to label someone as demonized, and why this gift of discernment of spirits is so important.

When I was in my third year at Southwestern College in Oklahoma City, a number of us went downtown on an outreach to the worst part of town, and there, in an alley behind the bus depot, we met Charlie. He was a large, intimidating guy, standing about six foot four. A few of us had been trying to witness to him, but he seemed agitated, and suddenly, looking straight at me, said, "You can't make me leave; this is my body!" Well, it didn't really take much discernment to tell what the source was that was working in Charlie. He was obviously demonized, and, after four hours in a deliverance session with a local pastor, Charlie was set free, received Jesus, and was filled with the Holy Spirit.

In Charlie's case it was easy to tell that he was demonized, but where the gift of discerning of spirits comes in really handy is when things are more subtle than that, which, in our culture, is most often the case.

One Sunday morning a man and his wife walked into our sanctuary and he introduced himself to me. On the surface, he seemed like a normal guy, but there was just something about him that made me very uneasy, and as I turned away from him, I found myself praying, almost without thinking, "Lord, please protect this church from him!" He never came back. I believe that the Spirit, that morning, had given me the gift of discerning of spirits.

My wife and I have had several similar experiences over the years, and I've come to believe that the Lord gives this gift quite often to pastors and leaders for the protection of His church.

Another time, at a conference at Westmont College in Santa Barbara, I was with a group of pastors, helping to minister to people who had come forward for prayer. The young woman that my friend, Steve Robbins, and I had been ministering to, had a visible protrusion from her stomach, which could easily have been mistaken for abdominal fat except for the fact that she was otherwise thin. After some time of prayer that really didn't seem to be going anywhere, Steve suddenly pointed at her stomach and said firmly, "Come out of her!" She cried out, "Oh!" and her body jerked once. As we continued talking with her, she pointed to her stomach and said excitedly, "My stomach's flat!" She had been delivered from a spirit that had afflicted her body because the Holy Spirit had given Steve the gift of discerning of spirits, right on time.

SPEAKING IN TONGUES GLOSSOLALIA

In the book of Acts, this gift, along with prophecy, was often the first gift of the Spirit that people exhibited, upon the infilling of the Holy Spirit (Acts 2:4; 10:44-46; 19:1-6). That was certainly true in my case. As I related earlier, when the Spirit fell on me in that little Pentecostal church in Fremont, California, in the summer of 1971, I burst out in a spontaneous torrent of tongues that seemed to last for 15 minutes (although, looking back, it was probably more like five minutes).

Ever since that day, speaking in tongues has been a big part of my life. Hardly a day goes by that I do not pray in tongues at some point, whether in my morning prayer time, or while walking, driving, or even while I'm in the checkout line at the supermarket (although under my breath in those instances). This practice has become almost as normal to me as breathing, and I have always found great benefit from it, as my faith seems noticeably strengthened during those times.

Evidently, this seems to have been Paul's experience as well. He confidently said to the Corinthians, which at the time was a church probably numbering in the thousands, *"I thank God I speak in tongues more than all of you"* (I Cor. 14:18). Then he hastened to add, *"But in the church I would rather speak five intelligible words to instruct others than ten thousand words in a tongue."*

On the Day of Pentecost, when the Spirit came upon the gathered disciples, they all spoke in *"other tongues as the Holy Spirit enabled them"* (Acts 2:4). Luke goes on to explain that they spoke in languages that were recognizable by many of those who heard them. Some, who are skeptical of speaking in tongues today, use this scripture to support their argument that any speaking in tongues should be in a recognizable foreign language.

There are two things wrong with this argument: First, there are thousands of languages and dialects spoken around the world today. So, just because someone doesn't understand what someone is saying when he/she speaks in tongues, that means very little. Even the most proficient linguists have usually only mastered a handful of languages. Second, in First Corinthians 13:1, Paul makes reference to "tongues of angels." It may very well be that in many cases (perhaps even in most cases), when someone today speaks in tongues under the inspiration of the Holy Spirit, he/she is speaking in an angelic language.

Many have spoken of tongues as "the least of the gifts," and have discouraged millions of believers from seeking this gift. But make no mistake—speaking in tongues is a wonderful gift from the Holy Spirit, and a vital part of your spiritual equipment. The only time Paul curtailed the use of this gift was when he was giving guidelines for its use in church gatherings. But even then he said, *"...do not forbid speaking in tongues"* (I Cor. 14:39).

There are so many times when we don't know how to pray, but we can easily pray perfect prayers by means of this gift. If you do not speak in tongues, let me encourage you to ask the Lord for this gift, and to keep asking until you get it! In my experience, there have been very few people who earnestly wanted this gift who did not receive it. Our God is a generous God!

Gordon Fee has written an excellent treatment of this subject in his book, *Paul, the Spirit, and the People of God.* Following is his most helpful summary of the gift of tongues:

1. Whatever else, it is Spirit-inspired utterance; that is made plain by First Corinthians 12:10 and 14:2. This in itself should cause some to speak more cautiously when trying to "put tongues in their place" (usually

meaning eliminate them altogether) in the contemporary church. Paul does not damn tongues with faint praise, as some have argued, nor does he stand in awe of the gift, as the Corinthians had apparently done—and some contemporary proponents of tongues do. As with all Spirit-empowered activity, Paul held it in high regard in its proper place.

2. The regulations for its community use in 14:27-28 make clear that the speaker is not ecstatic or out of control. Quite the opposite: the speakers must speak in turn, and they must remain silent if there is no one to interpret. Therefore the mind is not detached; but it is at rest and "unfruitful."

3. It is speech essentially unintelligible both to the speaker (14:14) and to other hearers (14:16), which is why it must be interpreted in the assembly.

4. It is speech directed basically toward God (14:2; 14-15;28); one may assume, therefore, that what is interpreted is not speech directed toward others, but the "mysteries" spoken to God.

5. As a gift for private prayer, Paul held it in the highest regard (14:4,5,15,17-18; cf. Rom. 8:26-27; Eph. 6:18).[11]

INTERPRETATION OF TONGUES (*ERMENEIA GLOSSON*)

The Greek word used for this gift can also mean "to interpret" or "to put into words." So when one interprets for someone who just spoke in tongues, the interpretation does not have to match, word for word. In other words, if someone speaks in tongues for 30 seconds, the interpretation will not necessarily be exactly 30 seconds, just like when someone interprets any language to another person or to an audience.

The important thing is that they accurately give the true sense of what was spoken.

This gift is the only one of the gifts that is dependent on another gift (tongues). However, it is important to be reminded that this gift, also, is a gift of the Spirit, and therefore only functions under the inspiration of the Spirit, as do all the other gifts, and has value, precisely because it is given by the Spirit.

As Fee has suggested in his summary of tongues above, since speaking in tongues is "speech directed basically toward God," we should expect the interpretation also to be directed toward God, and not to the audience. This is true in both Acts and in First Corinthians, where speaking in tongues is described as prayer or praise. This would rule out any "message in tongues," which would be tongues directed not to God, but to people. Paul explicitly says, in First Corinthians 14:2, *"For anyone who speaks in a tongue does not speak to men but to God."*

In my early years, growing up in Pentecostal churches, I would often hear someone speak in tongues in a church service, followed by an "interpretation" as a message to the people from God. I don't doubt that the interpreter was often inspired by the Holy Spirit. However what they were giving was probably not the interpretation, but a prophecy. Why would God need two gifts (tongues and interpretation) to accomplish what one gift (prophecy) could do by itself? So the point is not that a "message in tongues" is invalid, just that it has been mislabeled.

From what Paul says, in First Corinthians 14, interpretation is not necessary when someone speaks in tongues in private, but only when someone speaks in tongues in a church setting, so that everyone may benefit from what is said. In First Corinthians 14:16, Paul says, *"If you are praising God with your spirit, how can one who finds himself among those who do not understand say 'Amen' to your thanksgiving, since he does not know what you are saying? You may be giving thanks well enough, but the other man is not edified."* Again, Paul is saying that tongues is directed to God.

Please keep in mind that in order for a church to benefit from a study of spiritual gifts, at some point there has to be a place for their exercise, whether in a church service or home group. Dr. Peter Wagner has said, "All the good theories in the world about spiritual gifts will not be worth more than a pleasant head trip if their dynamics are not released for effective operation in local congregations."[12]

ENDNOTES

1. Notice that in Romans 12:3-5, just before Paul lists the various gifts, he says things like, "Do not think of yourselves more highly than you ought," and "... the members do not have the same *function*," and "... each member belongs to all the others." His emphasis is on humility, function, and mutual appreciation. This is similar to what he says in First Corinthians 12:27-31, with a slightly different nuance. There he says "God has appointed" certain people for different functions.

2. Jack Hayford, *Hayford's Bible Handbook* (Nashville: Thomas Nelson, 1995), 351, 383. Jack Hayford makes a good case for each of the three gift passages being a distinctive work of different members of the Trinity. He attributes the gifts of Romans 12 to the Father ("God gives"), the gifts of Ephesians 4 to Jesus ("It was He [Jesus] who gave some to be apostles, some to be prophets, some to be evangelists, and some to be pastors and teachers"), and the gifts of First Corinthians 12 to the Spirit.

3. James D.G. Dunn, *Jesus and the Spirit* (Philadelphia: The Westminster Press, 1975), 211.

4. The Greek reads "gifts of healings." Some interpret this to mean that the Spirit gives to many the various healings they need; others say that what is meant is

that the Spirit grants to different individuals various gifts to heal specific ailments.

5. This is a quote by John Wimber, the founder of the Vineyard movement. At one point in his ministry, John felt God had led him to teach about healing; and for about 10 months, Sunday mornings and Sunday evening, that is what he did. After the message, he would invite people who needed prayer to come to the front, and his leaders would then pray for them. They did this for about 10 months without a single person being healed. Then, one Monday morning, after a particularly frustrating Sunday, he was called on to pray for a woman who was sick in bed, and she was immediately healed! This opened a torrent of healing in and through John Wimber and his church, the Anaheim Vineyard. I was personally healed at the Anaheim Vineyard in 1985, after suffering with chronic sinusitis for over 12 years.

6. I recommend attending a healing conference by Mike Flynn, founder of FreshWind Ministries. Mike has conducted over 500 conferences around the world and has a very down-to-earth, scripturally sound, and enjoyable style. He can be contacted at mkfln@aol.com.

7. Heidi and Roland Baker, *Compelled by Love*, 47.

8. Gary S. Greig and Kevin N. Springer, *The Kingdom and the Power* (Ventura, CA: Regal Books, 1993), 394.

9. Ibid, 395.

10. Dunn, 229.

11. Fee, 169.

12. Peter Wagner, *Your Spiritual Gifts Can Help Your Church Grow* (Ventura, CA: Regal Books, 1979), 243.

Chapter 8

THE TREASURE IN THE MIDDLE

*"Our lives must be living incarnations of the love of
Christ Jesus if we will ever have an effective ministry."*
—Heidi Baker

AN INTERESTING THING HAS BEEN happening to me the last few
years. I have perhaps never been so intent on pursuing the Person of the Holy Spirit, to discover Him in many ways that I
have not known Him before, and to see Him through new eyes
as I notice hundreds of scriptures that refer to Him, which I
never really noticed before. I have marveled at Him as I learned
to marvel at Jesus, and as I marveled at the Father, once I was
introduced to His heart of love for me as my true Father.

Yet, at the same time, I have been led to yearn for a new
capacity to love. As I have discovered the deficit in my love for
my wife, for my church, and for lost people, I have cried out
to God to teach me how to truly love like He loves. Because
I know that when I finally stand before Him, He will not be
impressed by my anointing, my healing successes (which are
so greatly outnumbered by my failures), or how many times
I fell, shook, laughed, or trembled in His Presence. The only

thing that will count on that day is whether I learned to love. I am also motivated to cry out for His love by a world that is in greater pain than I have ever seen. Because, more than anything, it is the love of God that this world needs from me. And from you.

I must be careful here. I have spent a good part of this book so far, sharing with you my passion for the Holy Spirit, that blessed Wind of God that brings life-imparting change to everyone and everything He touches. My heart's desire is that you and all who read this book would capture a fresh excitement and yearning for all that the Spirit wants to do in and through you. I do not intend here, to diminish in the slightest way the high regard in which I hold the Spirit's gifts and activity. Hopefully you have already captured my heart for Him to some degree.

What I need to do here is exactly what Paul did, when he was inspired by the Spirit to place the thirteenth chapter of his first letter to the Corinthians between chapters 12 and 14. Between his Spirit-inspired discussion of spiritual gifts in chapter 12, and his elaboration of the gifts of tongues and prophecy in chapter 14, he wrote the most eloquent and powerful chapter about love in the entire bible.

So what's the message? The message from God is that there needs to be no competition between the activity of the Holy Spirit and an emphasis on love; we don't have to choose between the gifts or the fruit of the Spirit. These three chapters show us that the subject of the Spirit's gifts and the subject of His love have to be married. These two truths go together, like a delicious slice of steak between two fresh pieces of bread. Just like the two slices of bread with the steak in the middle create a steak sandwich, so the two chapters about the Spirit's activity, with the chapter of God's love in between create a "love sandwich."

God does not do these things haphazardly. He was completely intentional in this design, so we must ask "why?" Why is it so important that when we discuss this magnificent subject of the Holy Spirit and His activity in our lives, that we simultaneously reflect on the importance of being loving people? I must confess that I have not always given love the emphasis it deserves when teaching about the Holy Spirit. I have often allowed myself to be so caught up in the excitement of the actions of this wonderful Person, that I have sometimes presented an unbalanced focus on the gifts, while neglecting the beautiful fruit of love.

In looking for a model of a ministry that combines power with love, we need to look no farther than Jesus. Again and again, we read that Jesus was "moved with compassion," then went on to heal. In John 11, before He raised Lazarus from the dead, we are told several times about His love. In verse 3, when Jesus first got the word about Lazarus' being ill, we read, *"So the sisters sent word to Jesus, 'Lord, the one You love is sick.'"* Then, in verse 5, we are informed, *"Jesus loved Martha and her sister and Lazarus."* Later, in verse 33, on His way to Lazarus' tomb, we are told that Jesus was deeply moved, and two verses later, that He wept. His tenderness toward this family was so obvious to the crowd, that they said, *"See how He loved him!"*

When Jesus talked with the woman at the well (John 4), the very act of engaging her in conversation was an act of love, because no other Jew, let alone a Jewish male, would be caught speaking with a Samaritan woman. Then He reached out to her and offered her the "living water," and let her know that He was fully aware of her troubled past (five husbands and now living with a man to whom she was not married). Yet there was no judgment in His voice, and she felt so drawn to Him that she brought her entire village to meet Him.

In the thirteenth chapter of John, we are told, *"Having loved His own who were in the world, He now showed them the full extent of His love,"* as He wrapped a towel around His waist and washed their feet. Then, in the last chapter of John's gospel, He lovingly reinstates Peter, who had just denied Him three times in one night.

John seems to be the one, more than any of the disciples, who was so overwhelmed by Jesus' love that he consistently referred to himself as "the disciple whom Jesus loved." Then, in First John, in the space of just the third chapter, he says these things about love: *"How great is the love the Father has lavished on us, that we should be called children of God!"* (verse 1). *"This is the message you heard from the beginning: We should love one another"* (verse 11). *"We know that we have passed from death to life, because we love our brothers"* (verse 14). And, *"This is how we know what love is: Jesus Christ laid down His life for us. And we ought to lay down our lives for our brothers"* (verse 16).

I miss Mother Teresa. If ever someone embodied the love of Jesus for the poorest of the poor, it was she. But God has given us another Mother Teresa, and her name is Heidi Baker (although, because of her humility, Heidi would probably be uncomfortable with the comparison). As mentioned in an earlier chapter, she, together with her husband, Roland, have ministered for years in the African nation of Mozambique, caring for thousands of homeless orphans and planting thousands of churches. They have seen more miracles and dramatic healings than possibly any other Americans on earth today. But their testimony is that the force behind their passion is the love of God. As the title of their book explains, they have been "compelled by love."[1]

Listen to some of Heidi's testimonies:

> I did not move to Mozambique with an action plan to save the country. My goal was not to start a revival. My vision was not to oversee thousands of churches. I came to learn to love, and I am still just at the beginning of that journey today. I am just

starting to learn how to love more. I believe this is my lifetime goal. I want to love God with everything within me. I want to love my neighbor as myself.[2]

The poor are my friends and my family. Village life is quite simple compared to Western culture. I love to camp in the mud-hut villages and enjoy the simplicity of the poor. We sing and dance into the night, worshiping our beautiful Jesus.[3]

I have watched countless times as the blind gain their sight. I am a witness nearly every week of my life as the deaf are able to hear. I have seen people whose limbs were once crippled walk again in complete wholeness. I see thousands run to my Jesus. But...the simplicity of love healing a broken heart is what causes me to keep going.[4]

I'm a prisoner of love. I have given my life for love. It is joy unspeakable and full of glory. It's in every part of our journey here on earth. When babies die in our arms, there is a mourning deep within our spirits, but we know that the babies go straight from our arms into the arms of Jesus. Our hearts are comforted with this inexplicable joy. He just keeps on loving them in heaven, even more than we could here on Earth. In that is where we find our comfort.[5]

You are called to love the broken until they understand God's love—a love that never dies—through you. Yes, God wants you to do signs and wonders. But the love of God manifested through you is what people really need. So you must first see His face. You must become so close to His very heartbeat that you can feel what others feel.[6]

God is love. That means Jesus is love. That means the Holy Spirit is love. In our pursuit of the Holy Spirit and His awesome activity in our midst, let's never forget that, more than anything, more than power, healings, or miracles, it is the ongoing experience of His amazing love that we need to receive and to give. Because it is love, more than any other thing, that describes Him.

ENDNOTES

1. Heidi Baker, *Compelled by Love* (Lake Mary, FL: Charisma House, 2008).

2. Ibid, p. 17.

3. Ibid, p. 17.

4. Ibid, p. 37.

5. Ibid, p. 31.

6. Ibid, p. 32.

Chapter 9

THE RUDDER INSIDE

"Above all else, guard your heart, for it is the wellspring of life." Proverbs 4:23

BECAUSE THERE ARE THOUSANDS OF churches across America where pastors have little or no accountability structures, there has never been a greater need for men and women with good and trustworthy hearts. And make no mistake; pastors aren't the only ones at risk. I have lost track of how many people I've counseled over the past thirty-plus years, and I've discovered far too many times the ugly secrets that are hidden from public view. It is in the "inner parts"—the secret places of the heart— where a person's true character resides.

After David was confronted by the prophet Nathan about his sin of adultery and murder, he was filled with remorse and, sometime during that dark season of his life, he wrote the gripping Psalm 51. In verses 5 and 6 he said, *"Surely I was sinful at birth, sinful from the time my mother conceived me. Surely You desire truth in the inner parts...."* Then, a few verses later, he wrote, *"Create in me a pure heart, O God, and renew a steadfast spirit within me."* David knew the supreme value of a pure heart, of unhindered fellowship with his God, and during that "dark night of the soul," he yearned achingly for a return to innocence and intimacy.

GOD'S PREPARATION OF OUR HEARTS

A good heart is not only the key to a healthy relationship with God, but your heart condition also dictates your capacity to receive truth and provides fertile soil for good fruit. In the parable of the sower and the soils, Jesus described the person whose life produces a bountiful harvest: *"But the good soil stands for those with a noble and good heart, who hear the word, retain it, and by persevering produce a crop"* (Luke 8:15). Like a veteran farmer, God constantly tills the soil of our hearts, so we can bear fruit for eternity. If we are to successfully navigate the waterways of the Holy Spirit, while maintaining integrity, we must cultivate this same passion for purity of heart.

God has always gone to great lengths to prepare the hearts of people before entrusting them with great things. In Genesis 37, Joseph had two vivid and powerful dreams, through which God revealed to him that he was destined for greatness. But first God arranged circumstances over the next twenty-plus years to test Joseph and prepare his heart before the promise was fulfilled.

First, Joseph was sold as a slave by his brothers, then he was falsely accused of attempted rape and imprisoned in Egypt. Years later, after he had come to power and his brothers were reunited with him, his gracious treatment of them proved that God's work of refining his heart had done its job. He bore no resentment, but said to them, *"...Do not be distressed and do not be angry with yourselves for selling me here, because it was to save lives that God sent me ahead of you...to preserve for you a remnant on earth and to save your lives by a great deliverance"* (Gen. 45:5-7). Through all his trials and temptations, Joseph's heart was intact!

In First Samuel 16, the prophet anointed David to be the next king, and immediately David spent years fleeing for his life from Saul and enduring great hardship before the time was right for him to become king. Although Saul had mistreated him time and time again, and even tried several times to kill him, David never gave in to bitterness or revenge. In fact, when he heard that Saul was dead, he fasted and wept. It was through these trials that God was preparing his heart for greater things than he ever imagined.

Jesus Himself had to endure the same kind of testing and preparation of heart when the Spirit led Him into the desert to be tempted by satan, and then for the next three years as His own people rejected Him. It was evident that His heart had been unstained and free of bitterness as His tortured body hung on the cross and He begged the Father, *"Forgive them, for they do not know what they are doing"* (Luke 23:34).

SAUL AND DAVID—A CASE STUDY

In all of scripture, there is probably no more stark contrast between two hearts than the story of Saul and David, and probably no more explicit lesson in the importance of guarding your heart during times of testing.

The story begins in First Samuel 10, with the prophet Samuel anointing Saul to be the first king of Israel. As part of his equipment to lead God's people, we are told in verse 9, *"...when [Saul] had turned his back to leave Samuel, God gave him another heart..."* (Amplified Bible). So here is Saul, with a fresh anointing and a new heart, ready to lead the nation of Israel. But tragically, over the next few chapters, Saul fails two critical tests, and God rejects him as king.

In the first test, Samuel had commanded Saul to wait at Gilgal, before attacking the Philistines, saying, *"I will surely come down to you to sacrifice burnt offerings and fellowship offerings, but you must wait seven days until I come to you and tell you what you are to do"* (I Sam. 10:8). So Saul went down with three thousand soldiers, and waited at Gilgal for seven days. During this time his troops became increasingly fearful, and finally, when Samuel didn't show up on the seventh day, some of them began to leave. In desperation, Saul offered the sacrifice himself, in blatant disobedience to the word of the Lord through Samuel, who showed up just as the sacrifice was ending.

Samuel confronted Saul and said to him, *"You acted foolishly. You have not kept the command the Lord your God gave you. If you had He would have established your kingdom over Israel for all time. But now your kingdom will not endure; the Lord has sought out a man **after His own heart** and appointed him leader of His people..."* (I Sam. 13:13-14, emphasis mine).

In chapter 16, God sends Samuel to the house of Jesse, in Bethlehem, to anoint one of his sons as the next king over Israel. When he arrives, Samuel has Jesse parade his sons in front of him, beginning with the oldest, Eliab. Samuel was immediately impressed with Eliab, and thought, *"Surely the Lord's anointed stands here before the Lord."* But the Lord said to Samuel, *"Do not consider his appearance or his height, for I have rejected him. The Lord does not look at the things man looks at. Man looks at the outward appearance, but **the Lord looks at the heart"*** (emphasis mine). Finally, David is sent for, and the Lord directs Samuel to anoint him.

In the very next chapter, Israel and the Philistines gather for war, and Goliath makes his challenge every day for forty days, while the army of Israel runs from him in fear. When David shows up, bearing gifts from his father for his brothers and their officers, he is appalled at the situation, and livid that some *"uncircumcised Philistine"* would dare to *"defy the armies of the living God"* (verse 26). His comments are overheard, and he is brought to Saul. David says to the king, ***"Let no one lose*** *heart* on account of the Philistine; your servant will go and fight him" (verse 32, emphasis mine). You know the rest.

David's life is a case study of a man whose heart is fully devoted to God, and who does not allow his fear of people to trip him up, as Saul did. Meanwhile, Saul's heart condition continues to deteriorate, as he makes one bad decision after another, and we are told, in First Samuel 28:5, "*When Saul saw the Philistine army, he was afraid; **terror filled his heart**" (emphasis mine). Because God no longer answered him, he resorted to consulting the witch of Endor, and eventually his life ends on the battlefield, as he commits suicide.

The tragedy of Saul stands in dramatic contrast to the long and successful reign of David, and we are told again and again, that the defining issue for both of them was the condition of their hearts. Even though David later committed a serious sin in the case involving Bathsheba (II Sam. 11), he quickly repented when confronted by the prophet Nathan, and for generations to come, God compared subsequent kings to the standard set by David.

He Must Become Greater, I Must Become Less

These of course were the words of John the Baptist in John 3:30, when his followers became concerned that the crowds were going over to Jesus (NIV). The Amplified version adds some texture here with the translation, "*He must grow more prominent; I must grow less so.*" John understood that Jesus was exactly the right person for the crowds to follow, and that his role, all along, had been that of one who merely pointed the way to Jesus—only "*a voice calling out in the desert*" (John 1:23).

This issue—being at peace when another leader emerges, who begins to draw the crowds—touches something deep in every heart, and it tests us in at least three crucial ways: First, it forces us to deal with the temptation to become resentful, jealous, and bitter when our prominence is threatened. That is the way Saul chose. Is that the way we will go in that inner secret place of our heart, or will we be gracious and humble, and truly seek God to see if this new "hero" is part of His plan, and perhaps even our replacement?

Can we arrive at the place where we truly seek the person's success and even pray for it, as did Jonathan, when David seemed destined to take his place as Saul's successor? (Now, of course, we should always pray for discernment in these cases. Individuals will often show up who seem impressive in some way, and we shouldn't be in a hurry to abdicate our ministry, or to assume God has sent them to replace us. But we should always ask the Lord to help us guard our hearts.)

Second, it also surfaces in the pockets of insecurity that reside in most of us. Have we become dependent on people to give us a sense of our value? Have we become overly dependent on their support, financial or otherwise? Do we truly know, deep down in our hearts, that our strength, resources, and significance come, not from people, but from our heavenly Father?

If this touches something in you that is unresolved, let me encourage you to discover the tender, passionate, and all-encompassing love of the Father for you. Take some time to go on long walks and simply meditate on the love of Jesus for you, to get to know Him as your best friend. Drink deeply from passages such as First John and the Gospel of John, until you understand that God not only loves you, He likes you and wants to be with you all the time!

Third, we are also confronted with the issue of personal ambition. I used to think this was primarily an American issue, because of our addiction to "success," but I now know that this is a huge issue in every culture, because it is part of the fallout from the original meltdown in the Garden of Eden. What pastor has not battled the desire for recognition and the increase of his ministry, rather than the untainted advance of someone else's Kingdom—the Kingdom of God? What worship leader or musician has not struggled with the desire to perform for applause, rather than the simple beauty of leading God's people into His presence?

These are not peripheral issues. They go to the very root of our motivations and clearly affect the purity of our hearts. If we are to see the greatest awakening in history, there will need to be men and women of character in the lead. I believe God has been preparing a generation of men and women to do just that. May we often pray David's prayer from Psalm 139:23-24: *"Search me, O God, and know my heart; test me and know my anxious thoughts. See if there is any offensive way in me, and lead me in the way everlasting."*

Chapter 10

THE HOLY SPIRIT AND WISDOM

*"Wisdom is supreme; therefore get wisdom. Though
it cost you all you have, get understanding."*
Proverbs 4:7

WHEN BILLY GRAHAM WAS CONDUCTING his famous crusades
around the world, he would always have one of his team members precede him into his hotel room, just in case a woman
had gained entry in order to seduce him. This was wisdom in
action. He knew that if he had allowed himself to fall prey to
any scheme like this, even once, his fruitful and powerful ministry would be over. We should all be thankful that Billy had
the wisdom and discretion that gave him a 60-year ministry,
which continues to bear fruit all over the world.

In my lifetime, I have watched with dismay as one Christian leader after another has fallen victim to one of satan's
destructive schemes. In most cases, it has been adultery, but in
others it has been greed or pride or simply a lack of wisdom in
some area that has derailed their ministries. Sometimes leaders
don't fall into obvious sin, but become so consumed with their

ministries that their marriages and families suffer devastating consequences.

In his book, *The Emotionally Healthy Church*, Pete Scazzero relates the following story:

> In 1950 Bob Pierce founded what has become World Vision, the world's largest Christian relief and development agency. Today that organization serves more than fifty million people a year in 103 countries. Passionate for Jesus and for a world without hunger or disease, Bob Pierce began humbly, helping children orphaned by the Korean War. Every outreach he touched grew in size and scope. With unstoppable vision and energy he dreamed the impossible and then did everything imaginable to make it happen.
>
> Bob often prayed, "Let my heart be broken by the things that break the heart of God." That zeal drove him to the ends of the earth, marked by a seemingly inexhaustible passion to meet spiritual and human needs wherever he saw them.
>
> Unfortunately, his approach had disastrous consequences for his family. As one family friend stately politely, Bob's wife, Lorraine, "knew deprivation of a different kind than those to whom her husband was ministering."
>
> The stark reality is that he all but abandoned his own family. He had consistently put the opportunities for expansion and greater impact ahead of his wife and children. For example, when one of his daughters attempted suicide, she phoned him on one of his overseas trips and asked him to come home soon.
>
> "I just needed to feel Daddy's arms around me," she later explained.

Nothing required him to stay there in the Far East. He could have taken the next flight home. His wife pleaded with him to return. Instead, sensing the urgency and demands of so many people in need around him, he booked a flight to Vietnam.

"I knew he wouldn't come," his daughter later said. Several years later, she did successfully take her life.

Bob's relationship with his wife also deteriorated over time. At one point, years passed when they did not even speak. His relationships with his two remaining children were equally strained. By the final year of his life, at the age of sixty-four, Bob Pierce was alienated from everyone in his immediate family.[1]

In spite of many wonderful accomplishments, Bob Pierce left a very mixed legacy. Perhaps if he had pursued wisdom with the same passion he had to meet the needs of the suffering, his life would have looked very different. He may not have accomplished as much in terms of numbers, but he might have enjoyed the adoration of a strong family, and left behind a role model many could emulate.

According to the bible, of all the commodities that we can desire from God, wisdom is the greatest. Proverbs 4:7 says, *"Wisdom is supreme, therefore get wisdom. Though it cost you all you have, get understanding."*

When God appeared to Solomon in a dream and said, *"Ask for whatever you want Me to give you"* (I Kings 3:5), Solomon asked for wisdom. He said, *"...give Your servant a discerning heart to govern Your people and to distinguish between right and wrong"* (verse 9). His request so pleased the Lord that He gave him, not only wisdom, but also the things he did not ask for: long life and unimaginable wealth. God is always pleased when we seek wisdom.

The Holy Spirit showed up like a violent wind at Pentecost, and for a while the church enjoyed explosive growth. But, as is so often the case when the Holy Spirit comes, that's when things became complicated. We are told, in the sixth chapter of Acts, that the Hellenistic Jews (those Jews who had moved there from the Greek-speaking countries) became upset with the Hebraic Jews (those who were native to Israel), because their widows were being discriminated against in the food distribution.

The apostles recognized the severity of the problem, but also knew that God had a solution. They called a meeting of the entire fellowship of believers and instructed them to elect seven men who were *"full of the Spirit and wisdom"* (Acts 6:3) who would have the responsibility of dealing with the administration of this issue (interestingly, all seven of the men they elected had Hellenistic names). The apostles had exercised wisdom in this decision, and they insisted on wisdom in those elected to serve. When the Holy Spirit is at work, when the Wind begins to blow, wisdom must always be part of the rudder.

The presence and powerful working of the Holy Spirit does not negate the need for wise planning, healthy infrastructure, mature leadership, sound teaching, and intentional discipleship. If what we desire is not just a short-lived burst of spiritual excitement, but a long-lasting, world-changing awakening, substantially free from scandals, distractions, and foolishness, we must have wisdom from God.

Several years ago, our family traveled to Niagara Falls. As we stood at the rail overlooking the point where the water rushed continuously over the rocky edge, we were overwhelmed. For almost an hour, we stood there, transfixed, as the deafening roar and the mist surrounded us like a heavy blanket. The sheer volume of water and the intimidating sense of being confronted by raw power were truly awe-inspiring.

But that great power has to be channeled into the turbines that turn the generators, which provide electricity to millions of homes in Canada and the United States. Without years of careful planning, great expense, and hard work to put those generators in place, all of that power would go to waste.

It is the same with the power of the Holy Spirit. God provides the power, but we must exercise wisdom and create the proper channels for its flow. After the Holy Spirit came on the Day of Pentecost, three thousand people were baptized and immediately enfolded into home groups, where they were taught and strengthened in joyful fellowship. This is still a great model for the dynamic partnership than can exist between the Holy Spirit and wise followers of Jesus.

The Apostle Paul had more experience with the power of the Spirit than most people alive today. Throughout his lifetime, he had seen profound healings, miracles, and deliverances. God used him to reach thousands with the Gospel. He had even seen the dead raised. But in addition to all of this, Paul highly valued wisdom, and it showed, not only in his theological insight, but also in the way he developed the early infrastructure of the church. We read in Acts that Paul appointed elders in each of the churches he established, and most of those churches grew strong and continued to bear fruit for many years.

During the Wesleyan revival in England, John Wesley exercised similar wisdom in preserving the harvest by forming societies of new converts for discipleship and accountability, and by appointing lay ministers to travel and care for them. His well-thought-out system became famous and his method became known as "Methodism."

Wisdom is also reflected in how we structure our priorities. It's so easy to let ourselves get caught up in the demands of our "to-do" lists, or the priorities of other people, and to neglect our relationships with our families, or worse, our relationship with the Lord. This will not get easier as the harvest increases. Unless we have firmly established healthy boundaries, which include always giving ourselves first to God on a daily basis, it will get worse. We must seek God's wisdom and discipline to say "no" to some opportunities, or we will get buried by the demands of ministry and burn out prematurely.

Jesus demonstrated this kind of wisdom perfectly, right after He had spent the previous evening healing many in Simon's village. Luke tells us, in Luke 4:42, *"At daybreak Jesus went out to a solitary place. The people were looking for Him and when they came to where He was, they tried to keep Him from leaving them. But He said, 'I must preach the good news of the kingdom of God to the other towns also, because that is why I was sent.'"* He had spent time alone with the Father, and was refreshed in the scope and rhythm of His calling, so it was easy for Him not to be sidetracked by the pressing needs around Him.

Jesus also knew how to budget His time well, finding the perfect balance between teaching the multitudes, spending time developing the future leaders of His church, and retreating into those precious times alone with the Father. What was true of Jesus is also true of us: *"By wisdom a house is built and through understanding it is established"* (Prov. 24:3).

My favorite story about Jesus displaying wisdom is found in Luke, chapter 20. This really is a great "gotcha" story! Here's what Luke says:

> *Keeping a close watch on Him, they sent spies, who pretended to be honest. They hoped to catch Jesus in something He said so that they might hand Him over to the power and authority of the governor. So the spies questioned Him: "Teacher, we know that You speak and teach what is right, and that You do not show partiality but teach the way of God in accordance with the truth. Is it right for us to pay taxes to Caesar or not?"*

> *He saw through their duplicity and said to them, "Show Me a denarius. Whose portrait and inscription are on it?"*

> *"Caesar's," they replied.*

He said to them, "Then give to Caesar what is Caesar's, and to God what is God's."

They were unable to trap Him in what He had said there in public. And astonished by His answer, they became silent (Luke 20:20-26).

Don't you just love it? Here were these arrogant and hypocritical religious leaders and their spies trying to trap Jesus in His words, and He so beautifully and smoothly evades the trap, leaving them frustrated and outsmarted!

The reason I share this story with you is that this is exactly the kind of wisdom we are going to need in the coming revival. When God pours out His Spirit and the harvest begins pouring in, don't think for a minute that satan is going to take it lying down. He will mobilize his own spies and agents in the media (perhaps even in Christian media) to put us on the spot and try to catch us off guard, with the goal of undermining our credibility and making us look like fools.

This danger is so real that it cannot be overemphasized! Many of us have been crying out for God to pour out His Spirit on our nation, but with such an outpouring will inevitably come greater scrutiny. When that time comes, rather than reacting to every critic, or jumping at every invitation for interviews or news coverage, we need to be in constant and intimate fellowship with Jesus and the Spirit as the only reliable "Counselors" in these matters. That is the only way we can have confidence that we are saying the right things at the right time, in the right way to the right people.

"Wisdom is supreme; therefore get wisdom," says Proverbs 4:7. So where and how do we get it? I have found at least four ways that wisdom comes to us: First, we can become wise simply through the long journey of life's experiences. I say "can," because wisdom doesn't always come with age. We only learn

from our mistakes as we reflect on them and learn to avoid repeating them.

I'm reminded about the successful businessman who was approached by two young, ambitious wannabees. "What's the secret to your success?" they asked. "Two words," he replied, "right decisions." "Well, how do you make right decisions?" they persisted. "One word," he replied, "experience." They pressed him, "Okay, but how do you get experience?" "Two words," he said, "wrong decisions."

Among those whom God will use most effectively in the coming awakening will be seasoned men and women who have lengthy resumes, not only of successes, but also plenty of mistakes that they have learned from over time.

Second, wisdom is available simply by asking God for it. James tells us, in James 1:5, *"If any of you lacks wisdom, he should ask God, who gives generously to all without finding fault, and it will be given to him."* Then he goes on to say, *"But when he asks, he must believe and not doubt, because he who doubts is like a wave of the sea, blown and tossed by the wind. That man should not think he will receive anything from the Lord...."* Trusting in the goodness and generosity of God is the key to asking with confidence. But we are also told to ask persistently, and not to give up, to *"look for it as for silver and search for it as for hidden treasure..."* (Prov. 2:4).

Third, wisdom is found in the vast gold mine of God's word, the bible. Listen to the words of the Psalmist: *"Your commands make me wiser than my enemies, for they are ever with me. I have more insight than all my teachers, for I meditate on Your statutes. I have more understanding than the elders, for I obey Your precepts"* (Ps. 119:98-100). The bible is our vital source of wisdom because it is the book of the Spirit. As you search the scriptures, you are listening for the voice of the Spirit through His word, for He is called the "Spirit of Wisdom" (see Isa. 11:2 and I Cor. 1:17). Let me encourage you to cry out for a hunger and thirst for God's written word, and that you would understand it through the insight of the Holy Spirit.

Finally, it bears repeating that wisdom is found by pursuing Jesus. Paul prays, in Colossians 2:2-3, "*...that they may know the mystery of God, namely Christ, in whom are hidden all the treasures of wisdom and knowledge.*" ALL the treasures! Pursuing Jesus is the wisest thing you can do. Making time regularly to just be with Him, talking to Him, asking Him questions, worshipping Him, is always time rewarded.

ENDNOTE

1. Peter Scazzero, *The Emotionally Healthy Church* (Grand Rapids, MI: Zondervan, 2003), 39-40.

Chapter 11

THE SPIRIT AND THE MISSION

"You will receive power when the Holy Spirit comes upon you, and you will be My witnesses..."
Acts 1:8

IT'S BEEN ABOUT 8 YEARS since I met Bobby at the Toyota dealer, but I'll never forget his story. He was the only Assyrian I'd ever met. I didn't even realize they still existed. I figured they were an ancient civilization that had ceased to exist, or had been subsumed into some other culture, but here he was—a real, live Assyrian. He was the first salesman to greet me when I was looking around the lot. Bobby was very friendly, courteous and patient, but what got my attention was the interest he showed in the fact that I was a minister.

When we finally had the paperwork completed and were just sitting there, waiting for the finance office to get their stuff done, Bobby began telling me his story. Some time back, his brother-in-law had tried telling him about Jesus, and had been trying to get him to go to his church, but Bobby had been reluctant. He told me that before he left his brother-in-law's house that night, his brother-in-law told him that God was going to show Bobby a sign that would confirm the message about Jesus. I don't know how he knew Bobby would see a sign, but I assume the Holy Spirit spoke to him and prompted him to tell Bobby.

Anyway, Bobby went on to tell me that the next day, as he was pulling into the parking lot of the dealership he worked with at the time, there was a guy standing at the entrance holding a (literal) sign, that said, "John 3:16." He had no idea what it meant, but he asked one of the other salesmen if they had seen the guy with the sign, but when they looked outside, there was no one there. When he told some of the other salesmen about it, one of them said, "Oh yeah, 'John 3:16' is the sign that guy with the rainbow-colored afro holds up at football games." Finally one of them told Bobby it was a scripture reference, and Bobby looked it up. To make a long story short, he ended up committing his life to Jesus, and when I met him he was contemplating getting baptized.

Because his brother-in-law was faithful to the mission Jesus assigned to all of us, Bobby will spend eternity in heaven. And that is the real reason the Spirit was given—not just to make us "shake, rattle, and roll," but to be witnesses. One of the last things Jesus said to His disciples in the upper room, right before He was betrayed, was that the Holy Spirit would testify about Jesus, and that we also must testify (John 15:26-27). Of course, the scripture most of us Charismatics/Pentecostals are most familiar with is Acts 1:8, quoted at the top of this chapter: "You will receive power...and you will be My witnesses."

Reaching lost people has always been the top priority of Jesus and the Spirit. In Luke chapter four, when we read about Jesus returning from the desert *"in the power of the Spirit,"* we read that He was handed the scroll of Isaiah in the synagogue of Nazareth. The very first thing He read was, *"The Spirit of the Lord is on Me, because He has anointed Me to proclaim good news to the poor"* (Luke 4:18).

In the fourth chapter of John, we are told in verse four, that Jesus *"had to go through Samaria."* Most commentators agree that the necessity of this route was not because it was the shortest way to go, but because the Spirit had planned His encounter with the Samaritan woman at the well, and the resulting salvation of an entire town.

Then in the three parables Jesus told in Luke 15—the lost sheep, the lost coin, and the lost son—He was, in fact, underlining, with three powerful strokes, the urgency of reaching the lost and the joy in heaven when they are found.

When the Holy Spirit is poured out in any sovereign move of God, one of the things we should expect is to see large numbers of unconverted people finding Jesus. Admittedly, that is not always the first phenomenon to occur at those times, because there is sometimes the need for believers to first rekindle a fresh passion and to experience anew the fire of the Spirit. But at some point there needs to be widespread evangelism happening as the Spirit enforces the passion of Jesus for the lost.

DOING IT RIGHT

I wasn't quite sure why I was driving the 2 ½ hours down to Laguna Niguel yesterday, other than I knew I wanted to enjoy the "fellowship of the Holy Spirit" with my friend, a pastor named Mike. I knew Mike had a similar passion for the Holy Spirit, and that he often hosts conferences with speakers who are well-known Charismatic leaders.

I expected to come up to the receptionist's desk and have Mike step out of his office and meet me, but I had a hard time even finding the front entrance, because there were three large buildings and lots of activity going on. I finally spotted Mike in the parking lot, wearing work clothes and carrying a box of old clothes into their warehouse. He gave me the tour, showing me a warehouse full of twenty-foot-high stacks of clothes that had been sorted and shrink-wrapped into large bundles by their bundling machine, ready for shipment to Africa.

As he was showing me around and introducing me to the volunteers who were sorting through the piles of donated items, there was already a line forming for the distribution of food for the needy. Mike knew some of them by name and stopped to talk with them, including one couple that he had just baptized.

Mike continued the tour, excited about the new, walk-in cold storage units that would enable them to receive perishable food, and the large thrift store, which enables them to raise some funds, but lamented that he still can't cover the mortgage.

We went on through another building where there was a ministry class in progress, through the prayer room and offices, and finally we left to go to the restaurant. Over lunch, Mike shared with me how he had started out as a missionary, and together with a friend, had started a movement of churches in Cambodia and Thailand that now has over 3,000 churches.

On the way home I realized why the Holy Spirit had prompted me to drive all the way down through L.A. traffic to the far end of Orange County and meet with Mike. He wanted me to see a real, live example of what it looks like when a person fully embraces the whole message of the Kingdom—a kingdom that includes both passion for the Holy Spirit and His gifts on the one hand, and evangelism and care for the poor on the other.

Over thirty-plus years of pastoral ministry, I have discovered that there are two things that will inevitably atrophy, unless we intentionally go after them: Evangelism and Spiritual gifts. The reason is not hard to find: Both of these things make us move out of our comfort zones, and both of these things involve risk, and we tend to avoid both discomfort and risk!

The first church I pastored was in Rosemead, California, a working-class area of Los Angeles. I was about 28, freshly graduated from Fuller Seminary in Pasadena, and trying to figure out how to reach people for Jesus. One day the office phone rang and the voice at the other end of the line was a guy even younger than I, from an organization called Christians In Action (CIA). He offered to come and present a class on neighborhood evangelism, then take us by the hand and show us how to do it.

Over the next year, three or four of us would gather at the church on Tuesday evenings and go door-to-door talking to people about Jesus. We used a simple door-opening technique about taking a survey, then launch almost immediately into John 3:16, etc. It was the most basic method you could imagine, but over the next year or so we prayed the "sinner's prayer" with over 100 people in their doorways.

We were lousy at follow-up, although we did manage to start one short-term bible study in a home. However, during that period of time, even though none of those people showed up on Sundays, the Lord doubled our church with new families. Established believers. Tithing believers! It taught me that the Lord is pleased with even our feeble attempts to reach lost people, and will richly bless those efforts.

REVIVAL AND EVANGELISM

One of the great things that happened during the historic revival at Azusa Street (1906 -1910) was that many individuals were profoundly touched by the Holy Spirit and launched out into evangelism and missions.

A young woman named Mary Rumsey was baptized in the Holy Spirit at Azusa Street in 1908 and felt called to be a missionary to Korea. She spent the next 20 years preparing, and in 1928 left for Korea. When Japan invaded Korea, she had to go back home to the U.S., but she left behind eight churches and ten ordained pastors to continue her work in Korea. At the end of the war, the Assemblies of God organized the churches into the Korean Assemblies of God, and started a bible school. One of the first students was a young man named Yonggi Cho, who started what would become the largest church in the world, with a current membership in excess of one million![1]

There were many others who were touched by the Holy Spirit at Azusa Street and were powerfully used by God in the following years. Some of these were instrumental in founding the Assemblies of God, which would become the largest Pentecostal denomination in the world, and the Church of God in Christ, which has become the largest black Pentecostal denomination. Both of these movements, along with others that sprang up in the aftermath of Azusa Street, have been used by God to plant hundreds of thousands of churches, and to bring millions of people into the Kingdom.

The Jesus Movement, a revival that began in California in the late 1960's and early 1970's, gave birth to three church movements: Calvary Chapel, Hope Chapel, and the Vineyard, which have become highly effective in church planting and evangelism. Jews for Jesus also traces its roots to the Jesus Movement, and this organization has helped many Jews find their messiah, Jesus.

It seems without question that whenever the Spirit moves with power, we can expect to see an increase in missions, church planting, and evangelism. This is what happened after the very first outpouring in Jerusalem on the Day of Pentecost. That first day over 3,000 people received Jesus, were baptized, and were added to the life of the Church. Not long afterward, another 2,000 were added in one day, and during that season, Luke tells us in Acts 2:47, that *"the Lord added to their number daily those who were being saved."*

I can totally relate to many who are passionate about seeking the Holy Spirit and the release of His gifts. Like them, I am easily stimulated and filled with joy at the sight of the Spirit falling in manifest ways upon people. I too love the words, the tingles, the jerks, the falling, the laughter, and even the "drunkenness" that sometimes comes when the Spirit is powerfully present in a gathering. But let's never forget that all of these things are only physical signs of His presence, and never the goal. Above everything else He does, the purpose for the Spirit is the Mission!

ENDNOTE

1. This story was related by Dr. Vinson Synan of Regent University at the Vineyard National Conference on July 14, 1997. Dr. Synan is a recognized authority on the history of Pentecostal and Charismatic movements around the world, and is currently Dean Emeritus at Regent University in Virginia Beach.

Chapter 12

THE PINNACLE AND THE PROCESS

Now to Him who is able to do immeasurably more
than all we ask or imagine, according to His power
that is at work within us, to Him be glory in the
church and in Christ Jesus for ever and ever! Amen.
Ephesians 3:20-21

THREE THOUSAND NEW PEOPLE POURING into the church in one day! Not to hear a special speaker. Not because a celebrity was there. Not because the church was giving away great freebies. But because they had been powerfully convicted by the Holy Spirit, baptized into the Church of Jesus Christ, and now couldn't stay away!

The account in Acts continues with a vivid description of vibrant community life, as these transformed men and women were enfolded into home groups and taught daily about the Kingdom of God by anointed apostles. As the Spirit softened their hearts and as Jesus captured their affections, they willingly parted with material possessions so that the poor among them could be taken care of. Their hearts and their energies were now oriented toward a new Kingdom, and the things of this life were simply losing their attractiveness. And the Lord added more and more people to their numbers every day as the Church exploded throughout Jerusalem!

What was going on here? The short answer is the Holy Spirit came. Came in power; came with a loud roar; came with fire! But the short answer doesn't explain it all.

The core of about 120 believers, including the eleven apostles, had shared a common experience for the past three years with Jesus; then after His resurrection they had spent ten days praying together daily; finally, the Holy Spirit came on the Day of Pentecost, filling them with power. There had already existed a powerful camaraderie, fueled by an absolute certainty that Jesus was alive and coming back, and that they had been commissioned to prepare the world for the new Kingdom. Into this highly flammable mixture, the flame of the Spirit was thrown and the resulting explosion carried an incomparable synergy and an unstoppable momentum that would change the world forever.

This amazing picture of the new Church that has been preserved for us in the second chapter of Acts is the most exciting account of church life recorded in the New Testament. Here we get to see the Church like a high-performance car, rumbling smoothly, firing on all eight cylinders. I am convinced that the Holy Spirit did not just give us this story to inspire us, but to give us clues about how great outpourings of the Spirit happen. I believe that God wants to reveal some priceless yet simple truths to us about the process involved in arriving at this pinnacle of the early church's history, and this chapter is an attempt to explore these truths.

THE PROMISE

I once heard Bob Jones, an old prophetic voice from Missouri, say, "Papa don't appreciate what he don't initiate!"

Another way of saying this is that one of the indispensable keys to the success of any venture is the fact that God has initiated it. This one item alone is so essential for us to understand, because church history is full of mistakes and fruitless endeavors that were undertaken simply because they seemed like good ideas at the time, but were not God's ideas.

The Holy Spirit didn't come just because a group of Christians had been praying for ten days. He didn't show up because somehow they had figured out the right combination of principles or "keys" and all of a sudden the lock just clicked open and out popped the Spirit. He came because hundreds of years earlier, through the prophet Joel and others, God had promised that he would send the Spirit. And God always keeps His promises. That's why Jesus told them, in Acts 1:4, *"Do not leave Jerusalem, but wait for the gift My Father promised...."* The Holy Spirit came because it was the right time in God's sovereign plan. God had to take the first step.

So, in our present situation, has God spoken about His desire to bring a great revival? I believe the answer is "yes." And I believe this, not so much because there have been numerous prophecies to that effect, but for the following reasons:

- The times are desperate, and only a great revival will rescue our nation and solve its problems.

- God is good, merciful, and compassionate, and cares about our condition.

- God loves lost people and wants them all to be saved (Luke 19:10, II Pet. 3:9).

- The Church is God's instrument to reveal His love, His goodness, and His glory (John 15:27; 17:20-21, Matt. 28:18-20).

- God's Spirit within us moves us to pray for the salvation of the lost.

- More people than ever seem to be doing this, which indicates that God has initiated the first steps toward revival. (Although greater prayer is still needed.)

- God always responds when we pray according to His will (I John 5:14-15, Rom. 8:26-27).

As in all transactions involving God and us, there is always a partnership. Just because God has promised something doesn't mean we can just sit idly by and do nothing. God always involves people in the working out of His plans. Someone has said, "Without Him, we cannot; but without us, He will not."

THE PRAYING CORE

In the late John White's book, *When the Spirit Comes With Power,* after concluding that "a major revival could be on the way," he asks the question, "What ought we to do?" Then he answers,

> Above all, we must pray. Indeed we must give our-selves to earnest and persistent prayer. What we term renewal is not enough. Dramatic evidences of divine power are of no importance in themselves. If renewal within the church is to fulfill God's purpose for it and if Christ is to be glorified, it must lead to a major evangelistic thrust. It must result in what was once called an awakening in society generally. Only an extraordinary outpouring of God's Spirit will accomplish that.
>
> [He goes on to add,] We must therefore plead for an outpouring of the Holy Spirit on Christian congregations.[1]

In a few days, I will be joining thousands of other believers from all over Southern California for a full day of prayer at the Rose Bowl in Pasadena. We will do this because we believe prayer makes a difference. We understand that God is sovereign, yet the amazing truth is that He can be moved by the prayers of people. As God declares in the famous scripture, Second Chronicles 7:14:

> *If My people, who are called by My name will humble themselves and pray and seek My face and turn from their wicked ways, then will I hear from heaven and will forgive their sin and will heal their land.*

Personally, I believe there is some value in large-scale, one-day gatherings such as the one I plan to participate in at the Rose Bowl, but my conviction is that the prayer that will ultimately bring the full-blown awakening God desires will look different.

If history is any clue, the great revival will most likely come as numbers of desperate men and women gather together all over the nation in small groups meeting in churches, homes, and apartments to pray for a great outpouring of God's Spirit. It was exactly such a small group of women fervently praying together for revival for several months in an apartment in Pasadena that preceded the historic Azusa Street revival in Los Angeles.[2]

Martin Lloyd-Jones was one of the 20th century's greatest preachers and writers. In his book, *Revival*, he tells about the great revival that broke out in Northern Ireland in the late 1800's. He reports how it began with one man, James McQuilken, who began to talk to two other men, and they began meeting together as they felt the call to prayer for the surrounding villages. Jones goes on to say:

> Believe me, my friends, when the next revival comes, it will come as a surprise to everybody, and especially to those who have been trying to organize it. It will have happened in this unobtrusive manner, men and women just slipping away quietly, as it

were, to pray because they are burdened, because they can not help themselves, because they can not go on living without it. And they want to join with the others who are feeling the same thing, and are crying out unto God.[3]

Then, in another of his books, *Joy Unspeakable*, Martin Lloyd-Jones writes about the great need for revival, and says this:

You and I are called upon not only to believe [for revival] but to pray to God without ceasing for it; to ask him to open the windows of heaven and to send down the Spirit, to pour him upon us, that he may fall upon us in mighty power.[4]

In almost every revival, both in scripture and in church history, prayer has played a vital role. When that praying core of 120 people gathered daily in Jerusalem before the Spirit came, they were simply preparing their hearts and getting on the same page as God. They didn't know exactly what to expect when the Holy Spirit came, but they knew Jesus had made it clear that they would soon receive this promise of the Father.

THE PREPARATION

During those ten days of prayer prior to Pentecost, Peter stood up and led the group in a very interesting activity. He shared how Judas had been disqualified because he betrayed Jesus, and felt that the scriptures indicated Judas was to be replaced. They prayed, cast lots, and ended up electing Matthias as the new twelfth apostle.

The reason that was so significant is that up to that point, Jesus was the only one to appoint apostles. Now here, the infant church takes over that function, with the conviction that the Lord, in partnership with them, had approved the move. The church, under Peter's leadership, was already stepping up to the plate and moving in its authority.

There are those who feel it was all a mistake, because you never hear of Matthias again. However, you don't hear of most of the other twelve guys either. Beyond that, in Revelation 21 John sees a vision of the New Jerusalem coming down out of heaven, with twelve foundations supporting the wall, and on the foundation were written the names of the twelve apostles (obviously Judas would not have been included, so we must assume Matthias' apostleship was affirmed in Revelation).

In addition to this important step of repairing the infra-structure gap created by Judas, after Pentecost when the church faced the challenge of the Hellenistic widows being overlooked in the daily food distribution, the apostles took on another infrastructure challenge (Acts 6). They discussed the situation and recognized that the Lord had called them to the unique and vital role of prayer and preaching, and oversaw the form-ing of the new group of seven administrators. As a result, we are told that the church continued to grow and prosper.

During the great revival of the eighteenth century, John Wesley also understood the need for a healthy organizational structure. He directed thousands of new believers into small discipleship groups, and in that way was able to conserve the fruit of the harvest.

It's not always possible to anticipate the infrastructure needs in advance of revival, and we should not fall into the trap of over-organizing something too early. Yet we can and should pray for wisdom and foresight in this area, and trust the Holy Spirit to guide us as He did the believers as they prayed, both before and after Pentecost.

THE POWER

The second thing God gave, besides initiating the whole Pentecostal outpouring in keeping with His Promise, was of course the Holy Spirit. The Spirit was the crucial catalyst for everything that followed in the book of Acts. One of the last things Jesus said to His disciples before He ascended into heaven was that they would receive power when the Holy Spirit came upon them.

The only thing that will turn this nation around and bring about the great harvest so many have been praying for is a massive outpouring of the Holy Spirit. There is no other answer for the daunting problems facing us, and no other answer to the hosts of wickedness behind them, than the power of God made manifest through the Holy Spirit.

In that sense, the situation is not too different from what it was in Jesus day. At that time He commanded them not to even leave Jerusalem before receiving power from heaven (Acts 1:4). He would no doubt say something similar to us. Perhaps something like, "Don't even try to bring about change in your city, much less your country, before receiving the power of the Holy Spirit." And just like then, we will not have to guess whether we have received the power or not. The fruit of the Spirit may grow slowly and quietly over time, but the empowerment of the Spirit does not come like that. There may not always be tongues of fire, and the building may not always shake, but both scripture and history testify to the fact that when the Spirit comes with power, dramatic changes happen quickly and profoundly.

THE PROCLAMATION

So far we've seen that God did two things in connection with the coming of the Spirit: He made a promise that He would send the Spirit, and He kept that promise by pouring out the Spirit on the Day of Pentecost. We've also seen that the disciples did two things: They gathered daily to pray and they made the simple preparations they felt the Spirit leading them to make.

The third thing the disciples did was to open their mouths and speak. God set it up perfectly for Peter: He created the noise, which drew the crowd (Acts 2:1-4). Then, when the onlookers were arguing and making fun of the disciples, Peter took the stage, along with the Eleven. Luke tells us, in Acts 2:14, *"Then Peter stood up with the Eleven, raised his voice and addressed the crowd."*

With the Holy Spirit powerfully upon him, Peter passionately persuaded the crowd that what they were seeing was God the Father, Jesus, and the Holy Spirit in action. As a result, they were deeply convicted, they repented and were baptized into the church.

While we are praying for God to pour out His Spirit, let's also pray for boldness to speak to people about Jesus. You may not know where to begin, but start by praying for God to create openings in conversations, or to set up divine appointments with people who need Jesus. Then keep your eyes open.

At this point, you may be among those who say, "But I don't have the gift of evangelism." And I would say, there is no such gift mentioned in the bible! The only gift that comes close is the office of evangelist in Ephesians 4:11, and some references to a few who were evangelists. But we are all called to reach lost people for the Kingdom.

Every pastor I know and virtually every commentator I've read believe that the Great Commission in Matthew 28:18-20 applies to every believer. I completely understand the intimidation that is felt when challenged like this, but I believe that timidity will largely disappear when the Spirit comes with power. Everything will change when the Spirit shows up, and those gifts that are dormant in you will be activated full blast! But you don't have to wait for the great revival; ask God to revive you now!

I must emphasize that we are not to just pray and wait for revival before we make any effort to reach lost people. As I shared in Chapter 1, in the absence of the Wind of the Spirit, we are still to row faithfully, doing the best we can with our available resources. Although rowing requires more effort, God is still pleased when we are faithful and obedient to His commands (such as the Great Commission). Let's keep rowing while we pray for the Spirit to come in power!

THE PEOPLE

The third thing God did was to send the people—three thousand the first day, and then many more in the days that followed, including another two thousand when Peter and John healed the crippled man (Acts 4). This is power evangelism! We are talking about the pinnacle, the greatest example of the Church operating at full capacity. When the Church is functioning at its peak Spirit-fullness, this is the kind of evangelism we can expect to see.

Psalm 24:1 says, *"The earth is the Lord's and everything in it, the world, and all who live in it."* Then Jesus said, in John 17:6, *"I have revealed You to those whom You gave Me out of the world. They were Yours; You gave them to Me and they have obeyed Your word."* These scriptures make it clear that every person on this planet belongs to God, and He can add them to the Church if we ask for them.

Now, obviously, God will send lost people to those who are properly equipped to take care of them and faithfully make disciples out of them. Which brings us back to the second step mentioned above, the preparation. If we are praying for a great harvest, let's begin practicing and honing our disciple-making skills now. Otherwise, when the harvest comes flooding in, many of us will be caught off-guard and much of the harvest could be lost.

ENDNOTES

1. John White, *When the Spirit Comes With Power* (Downers Grove, IL: InterVarsity Press, 1989) 225-226.

2. Morris and McCowan, 28.

3. Martyn Lloyd-Jones, *Revival* (Wheaton, IL: Crossway Books, 1987), 165-166.

4. Martyn Lloyd-Jones, *Joy Unspeakable* (Wheaton, IL: Harold Shaw Publishers, 1984), 279.

Chapter 13

Finding a New Normal

"The trouble with normal is it always gets worse."
—Bruce Cockburn

ONE OF THE THINGS I'VE discovered about human nature is that we are very attracted to comfort. That's why some guys have a hard time getting rid of those comfortable (but ugly and smelly) tennis shoes, even when they're falling apart and barely functional. It also explains why we get so comfortable with our familiar level of spiritual passion, that we're likely to stay there for years, unless something drastic happens to get our attention and move us to a new level.

It's so easy to get used to a certain way of living—so much sleep, so much work, so much leisure time, so much TV time, so much (or so little) prayer time, so much church, so much time helping others, so much time in God's word, etc. Each one of us inevitably settles in to a "normal" way of living, and we get comfortable with that. It's like becoming attached to that old pair of tennis shoes, or sitting in the same place in church week after week.

A few weeks ago, after spending four days of fasting and prayer on an isolated ranch, the Lord began speaking to me about the need to find a new normal. I believe this is a very time-sensitive word, not only meant for me, but for the Body of Christ. As I have reflected on this conviction, it seems to me there are two main reasons we need to find a new normal.

First, we are about to see a new awakening in this nation, greater than any revival in our history. I'm as sure about that as I've ever been about anything in my roughly 60 years on this planet. If indeed this is the case, we must rise to the occasion. We must step up to the plate. We must answer the call. We must raise the bar. However you phrase it, the thing that God has planned is so historic and so profound that the Church must get serious now about getting mobilized. That means that you and I, as individual members of the Body of Christ, need to begin seeking God about what His "new normal" is for us, because right now we are unprepared, and what has been normal for us is not going to cut it.

The second reason is this: The desperate condition of our nation, and of the other western nations, demands that the Church respond. There is already a "new normal" developing all around us, as we face new economic challenges and new threats (you may already have heard the term "new normal" used in this context). The world most of us grew up in is not the same world we will face in a few years. The only answer to the magnitude of the problems facing us is Jesus and His kingdom. And the Church has been given the privilege and responsibility of joining with the Spirit of God to rescue our communities, states, and nations in the power of God.

In Hosea, God spoke these words to the nation of Israel:

> *Sow for yourselves righteousness, reap the fruit of unfailing love, and break up your unplowed ground; for it is time to seek the Lord, until He comes and showers righteousness upon you* (Hos. 10:12).

While in this context the implication was that all of Israel was unfruitful, like hard, uncultivated ground, I believe there is a more encouraging application for us. Each of us has areas in our lives that are like hard, unfruitful ground, but God is saying that if we will begin to pay attention to those areas, cultivate them, and seek the Lord in a deeper way, we can see new and exciting fruitfulness in those places.

Let me illustrate from our recent gardening experience. We have a planter box that I created by building a two-and-a-half-foot high block wall when we first moved into this house eighteen years ago. We have occasionally planted flowers in most of this planter box that rings our backyard, but there has been the larger, wider part of the box on the side of our yard that has served as the dumping ground for a variety of junk.

About six months ago, my wife, Jane, asked me to clear that area and get the ground ready for a vegetable garden. It took two days to haul off the old, rusted lawnmowers, a broken down wheelbarrow, some old fencing, miscellaneous pieces of wood, and unwanted weeds. Then I began the hard work of digging up the ground with a pick-axe to a depth of about a foot. I had to break up the hard, clay-like clods into little pieces, tossing out rocks and pieces of debris. Then I added bags of sand to improve the texture of the soil. After that we added chicken manure, bone meal, blood meal, ash, and a bag of highly nutritious amendments, constantly mixing it up. In the process, I rediscovered a four-letter word: W-O-R-K!

When we were done preparing the soil, it looked amazingly transformed. (Actually I should say, "When *I* was done," since *I* was the one inside the box, while Jane told me what to do!) After that, she planted a variety of vegetables, including squash, peas, beans, tomatoes, peppers, and lettuce, which have grown rapidly and ended up on our table.

As I read the passage in Hosea above, the Lord reminded me of how we were able to transform that unused, cluttered area of our yard into something beautiful and productive. In the same way, I believe He is challenging us to examine our lives and let Him show us those places where we have allowed "junk" to accumulate and weeds to grow. In addition to that four-letter word I mentioned above, this will require another four-letter word: T-I-M-E. Time to read more wisely, time with people who can really help us move forward spiritually, and above all, more time in prayer. In the process, we may have to redistribute our time more wisely (perhaps less TV, etc.).

When I was driving back from that prayer retreat I mentioned earlier, the Lord began giving me one-word impressions related to finding a new normal. I'd like to share those twelve words with you in this next section, and encourage you to meditate on each of these powerful words. (All of this just happened a few weeks ago, so this is perhaps the freshest bread in the whole book!)

I have arranged these twelve words in three sections: our challenges; what we can do about the situation; and the payoff.

The following are elements of a New Normal, starting with our challenges.

OUR CHALLENGES

Homeostasis

Homeostasis is the tendency of something to revert to its previous condition. Like when you stretch a rubber band—it expands for a while, but when you let go, it returns to its previous size and shape. This is the resistance to change that each of us comes up against when beginning to pursue God in a new and deeper way. It's like the force of gravity, and we're like a rocket trying to escape its pull and soar into the "wild blue yonder."

Whenever you make a decision to change, there are always enemies lurking in the shadows. These enemies include your old habits, attitudes, beliefs, and deeply ingrained routines. They conspire to sabotage your determination to break free from their oppressive limitations, and many of us have encountered them when trying to establish our noble New Years' resolutions. But these forces are not omnipotent, as we shall see.

Distraction

We live in a very distracting age! Behind much of that distraction are spiritual forces with a very clear mission to keep us boxed into a self-absorbed lifestyle. They conspire with our "flesh" to keep us off-focus and ineffective, with regard to Kingdom priorities. Breaking through the limits imposed on us by all of the distractions takes a fresh determination and Spirit-inspired wisdom.

What are some things that may be distracting you from fully pursuing Jesus and His Kingdom? Could it be a relationship? How about a secret sin? Maybe it seems as harmless as too much TV, or maybe you have just let yourself become so busy with non-essential things, that it has left you with little or no time for eternal things.

Dissipation

This word means the wasting of something, such as "the dissipation of a fortune." In our context, we're talking about squandering our time, energy, and resources on things that have little or no real value, especially in terms of eternity. Closely related to distraction, dissipation is the unfortunate result of giving into these distractions. We need to take seriously Paul's exhortation in Ephesians 5:15-17:

Look carefully then how you walk! Live purposefully and worthily and accurately, not as the unwise and witless, but as wise (sensible, intelligent people), making the very most of the time [buying up each opportunity], because the days are evil. Therefore do not be vague and thoughtless and foolish, but understanding and firmly grasping what the will of the Lord is (AMP).

Jesus warned us, when talking about the time just before the end of the age, *"Be careful, or your hearts will be weighed down with **dissipation**, drunkenness and the anxieties of life..."* (Luke 21:34).

Most of us can easily recognize the obvious sins that are threats to the vibrancy of our walk, but we need to gain a fresh awareness of the "little foxes" that have the combined effect of sapping our time and energy, like holes in the purses of our lives.

Indulgence

This is a friend of dissipation and distraction. Indulgence is the act of giving into distractions and temptations, in order to satisfy our fleshly appetites. We all face different challenges and temptations, but for you this could mean illicit sexual activity, habitually overeating certain kinds of foods or sweets, drinking beyond moderation, or simply spending way too much time, energy, and money on TV, recreation, or sports.

Years ago there was a woman in my church who was in the habit of spending an inordinate amount of time reading romance novels. What began as a distraction eventually became an indulgence, which led to an obsession. She developed such fantasies that she eventually left her husband for another man. The tragedy is that she claimed to be a Christian, and we had been trying to win her husband to Jesus.

Please don't misunderstand: God made all things for us to enjoy, but He has placed healthy limits for our protection. I'm not suggesting you should give up everything that gives you joy or pleasure. I'm only inviting you to ask the Lord to help you establish a healthy balance for the purpose of seeking first His Kingdom.

This is probably a good place to also talk about the importance of taking time out for yourself. God thought it was so important for us to find a healthy rhythm between work and rest, that He made the Sabbath a commandment. Even though most of us don't hold religiously to Saturday as a day of rest, it's still important to take one day a week away from your work. If you don't do this as a lifestyle, the stresses of life will eventually catch up with you, and your attitude will begin to stink!

TWO THINGS WE CAN DO ABOUT IT

Now that we have seen the challenges we face in finding a new normal, here are two words that best encapsulate an effective response: Pursuit and Acceleration.

Pursuit

The best way to find a new normal is by pursuing Jesus like never before. Paul tells us, in Colossians 2:3, that in Christ *"are hidden all the treasures of wisdom and knowledge."* Jesus is the key to the Kingdom, but simply knowing this, even deeply, doesn't necessarily give us the power to change. We have to become pursuers of Christ, not settling for anything less than an uninhibited chasing after Him.

Successful pursuit is fueled by desperation. I recommend asking God for the gift of desperation, and for grace to seek His face with greater perseverance. We are promised, in Jeremiah 29:13, *"You will seek Me and find Me when you seek Me with all your heart."*

Acceleration

Just like a rocket burns up almost all of its fuel on lift-off, trying to escape the pull of gravity, so we need an extra amount of thrust when trying to escape the pull of our old normal and soar into the freedom of a new normal. I have found no better way to do this than three or more days of fasting and prayer. Fasting is one of the spiritual disciplines that has greatly bene-fited Christians throughout the centuries. It truly is a powerful weapon in your arsenal and is a great way to jump-start your new normal.

If you're new to fasting, try a partial fast, such as skipping one or two meals a day, and using that time to pray. Or fast all meats and sweets, etc. Or even begin with only juices for just one day. Once you've got the hang of it and realize that you survived, move up to three or four days or more. I guarantee this will accelerate the process of change.

I would also highly recommend finding a few friends or a small group in your church to join you in this adventure. It will help, like nothing else can, to keep you accountable and motivated past the "honeymoon" period, when the initial excitement has worn off. If you find, after the first three or four weeks, that you're having trouble maintaining your new nor-mal, think about another day or more of fasting and prayer. Above all, keep praying. Try praying at times other than, and in addition to, your normal prayer time.

THE PAYOFF

Revelation

We all face those desperate times in life when we need to know what to do. What do we do about that situation at work or about our career choice? What do we say to a loved one going through a crisis? How do we find the answers to these and many other of life's tough questions?

One of the amazing things that happen as part of a new normal is that we begin to see with new eyes, and we begin to understand with new wisdom, because the fog and confusion we have become so used to has cleared as we have drawn closer to God. How valuable is this? Let me share a story from Henry Ford's day.

Henry Ford is not only credited with inventing the first automobile, he also invented the assembly-line process, which contributed greatly to the industrial revolution. But things did not always go smoothly at his factory. As the story goes, one day there was a serious breakdown of a major piece of machinery that powered his assembly line. He called in the man who invented and built the machine, and after only an hour or two, the problem was fixed. A few days later, Henry Ford received a bill for $10,000.

Aghast and horrified, he demanded from the man, "It took you less than two hours to fix that machine, and the replacement part cost you less than a dollar! How could you charge me $10,000?" The man sent another bill, breaking down the charges as follows:

Cost for the part: $1.00.

Cost for knowing where to look: $9,999.00.

Ford paid the bill.

Revelation about the issues we face in life is part of the blessing of a new normal, but more importantly is finding new clarity and understanding about the ways of God. Paul writes, in Ephesians 1:17-19:

> *I keep asking that the God of our Lord Jesus Christ, the glorious Father, may give you the Spirit of **wisdom** and **revelation**, so that you may know Him better. I pray also that the eyes of your heart may be enlightened, in order*

that you may know the hope to which He has called you,
the riches of His glorious inheritance in the saints, and His
incomparably great power for us who believe.

To hear God more clearly, to better see what the Father's doing, to have greater insight into the meaning of scripture, to discern His will in given situations more accurately. Isn't this what we all want? These are the kinds of benefits that can accrue to those who step up to a new level of relationship with God—a new normal.

Attraction

We read over and over in the gospels that crowds constantly gathered around Jesus. One of the reasons people were drawn to Jesus was because He was full of the Holy Spirit, and the Holy Spirit is the most effective PR person in the universe!

Peter discovered that on the Day of Pentecost, as a crowd of thousands gathered. He found it happening again, as we read in Acts 5:15-16, which tells us:

...people brought the sick into the streets and laid them on
beds and mats so that at least Peter's shadow might fall on
some of them as he passed by. Crowds gathered also from
the towns around Jerusalem, bringing their sick and those
tormented by evil spirits, and all of them were healed.

When you embrace the challenge of a new normal, your Spirit-fullness will make you a people magnet. It may not solve all of your problems, but because you are living closer to the flame of the Spirit, God's favor on you will increase, and people will find you more enjoyable to be with.

Passion

The term "fanatic" is a matter of perspective. Some of the same people who deride passionate believers as fanatics seem to have no problem acting like fanatics at ball games. Have you seen the crazy pieces of paraphernalia that some of them wear? I'm talking about huge pieces of artificial cheese on their heads, or gruesome pirate masks on their faces, or face paint and body armor! And the way some of us carry on at those games, you would swear our very lives were at stake!

But, in reality, radical is normal in the Kingdom of God. Jesus was the epitome of a radical and revolutionary. He challenged the ruling powers, made a whip and overturned the tables of the money changers in the temple grounds, walked on water, spat on the blind man's eyes, and talked about people eating His flesh and drinking His blood!

Also, when asked what the greatest commandment is, He answered, in the words of Deuteronomy 6:5:

> *Love the Lord your God with **all** your heart and with **all** your soul and with **all** your mind and with **all** your strength"* (Mark 12:30).

Jesus considered it so important to be passionate that His most severe rebuke in the book of Revelation was for a church that showed a lack of passion. Read what He said to the church at Laodicea in Revelation 3:15-16:

> *I know your deeds, that you are neither cold nor hot. I wish you were either one of the other! So, because you are luke-warm—neither hot nor cold—I am about to spit you out of My mouth.*

One of the reasons people are attracted to those who are full of the Spirit is because people who are full of the Spirit are passionate. They may not always be on the right side about every issue, but they are seldom boring. I decided, a long time ago, that our mission is so important, and this life so brief, that to live any other way but full throttle is a sin! You will discover that one of the rewards of the new normal I'm talking about is an increase in passion.

Robustness

Sometimes, when people try to get closer to God, they become hyper-sensitive about being around sin and sinners, as if they might catch their sin, like the bird flu or some other virus, and mess up their spirituality. Yes, we definitely need to be smart about the movies we watch, or the books we read, and the things we say and do. But we should never be afraid to hang out with even the worst sinners (unless, of course, you're a new believer and haven't quite got your "kingdom legs" yet. We sure don't want to get you in trouble before your faith gets grounded!).

Jesus' relationship with His Father was strong and His identity was secure. As a result, you could always find Him hanging out with sinners. In fact, He was called their friend. A new normal will include a faith that is robust enough to withstand any sinful environment.

This issue also tends to surface when we're pursuing spiritual disciplines like prayer, fasting, reading scripture, etc. If your wife interrupts your quiet time and asks you to wash the dishes or vacuum the floor because your guests will arrive soon, probably the most spiritual, God-pleasing thing you could do, would be to put your bible down, get up, and help her. Remember, we're not going for an obsessive, hyper-spiritual faith, but a robust faith.

Extravagance

Several times in this book I have mentioned Hebrews 11:6, which tells us that God is a rewarder of those who earnestly seek Him. Over the past few years, as I have sought to practice the things I'm championing in this book, I have found that to be an understatement (which is actually very characteristic of God—He tends to undersell Himself). I have discovered that

God is far more generous, far more extravagant in His blessings than I could ever imagine.

But God not only wants to display His generosity to us, He wants us to emulate His generosity toward others. Read about the new normal the first Christians discovered, Acts 2:44-45:

> *All the believers were together and had everything in common. Selling their possessions and goods, they gave to anyone as he had need.*

Then, in Acts 4:32-34:

> *All the believers were one in heart and mind. No one claimed that any of his possessions was his own, but they shared everything they had...There were no needy persons among them. For from time to time those who owned lands or houses sold them, brought the money from the sales and put it at the apostles' feet, and it was distributed to anyone as he had need.*

You don't necessarily have to embrace that level of radical lifestyle at the beginning of your new normal, but think about beginning with the small things, like tipping generously. I make it a practice to tip at least 20%, no matter how bad the service was. You disagree? Think about what Jesus would do.

As you find a new normal, you will also begin to find extravagant joy, extravagant peace, and extravagant love. God doesn't do mediocre; He only does extravagant!

Actualization

The gist of this word is that when Jesus is with you, everything works! There are some profoundly extravagant scriptures in the New Testament! I call them, "scriptures of potentiality," because in them Jesus is describing things that can be ours. In this last section I want to briefly take a look at three of them, which are filled with untapped potential and through which you can begin to experience a new normal.

Matthew 15:26

In this passage, Jesus has been approached (actually hounded!) by a Canaanite woman who won't take "no" for an answer. In the course of bantering with her about why her daughter should or shouldn't be healed of an unclean spirit, He makes a clear inference, in verse 26, that healing is "the children's bread." Not an optional appetizer, not dessert or the icing on the cake, but the bread! Remember that in that culture bread was the staple of life. Healing has always been part and parcel of the new covenant that Jesus brought!

I believe that a new normal will include increased levels of healing (spiritual, emotional, and physical). There are many people, churches, and ministries today that are already experiencing this, such as the Healing Rooms movement and others. Jesus repeatedly modeled this for us and made astounding promises, like the one in the next example.

John 14:12

We've already discussed this scripture in Chapter 3, but to summarize, Jesus promised, *"Anyone who has faith in Me will do what I have been doing, and greater things."* Then, in the next breath (verse 13), He said, *"And I will do whatever you ask in My name, so that the Son may bring glory to the Father."* And just in case we didn't get it, He continued (verse 14), *"You may ask Me for anything in My name, and I will do it."*

Granted, the context of this passage is the works of Jesus, so He's not saying we can put in our order for a new Lexus SC 430[1] and expect it ASAP But He is promising that in His "normal," we can follow Him in doing the very healings and miracles He did, and even greater things. And we have seen in previous chapters, there are those who are already living in that new normal.

John 17:13

In this scripture, which was part of Jesus' prayer in the upper room just before He was betrayed, Jesus expresses the desire that we may have "the full measure" of His joy! He didn't say these kinds of things flippantly—this was His prayer to the Father! He really does want you to have the *full measure* of His joy, and, assuming you are not already living in that experience, it too can be part of your new normal.

There are many other promises and invitations Jesus talked about that most of us have not yet accessed. I don't believe there has been any reluctance on God's part, but there has been a great deal of doubt and hesitancy on our part. Isn't it time we simply started believing that our awesome God is as generous, as extravagant, as His word declares?

I invite you to join me and many others in these last of the last days before the return of Jesus, to find a new normal. Let's give the historians something new to write about—maybe "The Great Revival of 2015," or something similar. What have you got to lose? Isn't it worth it to just go all out for the Kingdom?

FINAL CHALLENGE

You and I are living in an incredibly exciting moment in history! More and more people and churches are beginning to discover the awesome joy and power of the Holy Spirit. There are historic changes and revivals sweeping across many nations, and it is my conviction, as well as the conviction of thousands of other Christian leaders, that the nations of the west are next in line.

God is recruiting leaders. This should be no surprise, because there seems to be a crisis of leadership in the secular world, leaving a vacuum that needs to be filled with men and women of integrity and Spirit-fullness. This is a time of opportunity for the Church of Jesus Christ!

The ship is about to leave the dock for the great adventure. The supplies are stored, the crew is at their stations, the sails and hardware have been checked, and the rudder is set for the course. Come aboard and sail with the Wind!

ENDNOTE

1. For those of you who may know, I do realize they don't make the little two-seat Lexus SC 430 anymore, but it's still one of my favorite cars, and destined to become a classic! (I'll probably have to settle for one that's 12 years old with 120,000 miles, but that would be okay, assuming God will want that to be part of *my* new normal!)

DISCUSSION QUESTIONS

CHAPTER 1

1. At the beginning of Chapter 1, Dan mentions two paradigms for ministry and life: One characterized by hard work, long hours of planning, etc., and the other characterized by a sense of partnership with the Holy Spirit, which is less demanding and more fruitful. Which of these would you say you live in most of the time?

2. Can you think of a time when you felt the Holy Spirit enter your situation and bring greater effectiveness or blessing?

3. Have you ever been in a situation where you felt God had given you a promise or sense of direction concerning something, but you had to wait for God's timing?

   • What was the outcome?

   • Are you in one of those situations right now?

   • If so, how do you feel you are handling the wait?

   • Do you have any sense of what God may be doing in you during this season of waiting?

4. This chapter discussed the concept of "letting go" of our agendas when we sense the Lord may want to do something unplanned. Can you think of a time this happened to you? How did you handle it?

   • If you can't think of a time you personally experienced this, can you recall a time in Jesus' ministry or elsewhere in scripture when He or someone else let go of the "plan" in order to follow the Spirit's leading?

5. Toward the end of the chapter, Dan talked about "finding the flow" of the Holy Spirit, where you experience inspiration and creativity. Have you had any occasions when this happened to you? If so, how did you find that flow?

CHAPTER 2

1. This chapter states that the Holy Spirit is a distinct Person, just like the Father and the Son. Do you ever pray directly to the Holy Spirit or worship Him? Why or why not?

   • How would you describe your relationship with the Holy Spirit?

2. Luke 10:21 tells us that Jesus, at that moment, was "full of joy through the Holy Spirit." What do you think that looked like?

   • Have you ever experienced the joy of the Holy Spirit or been in a situation where others did? How did it affect you?

3. Do you know someone in your church or community who seems "full of the Holy Spirit?" If you do, how would you describe their effect on you?

4. This chapter discussed the power of the Holy Spirit. What experiences have you had where you knew the power of the Spirit was present?

5. The life-giving power of the Spirit was another subject of this chapter. What do you think you and others in your church can do to see that life-giving quality demonstrated more powerfully?

CHAPTER 3

1. What is your interpretation of John 14:12?

2. This chapter began with how we experienced our childhood fantasies, and how that compares with our present experience of the Kingdom of God. What have you not yet seen God do that you would like to see in your lifetime?

3. The author gave several examples of people who "heard" God in various ways. How does God normally speak to you?

4. Discuss some of the ways people in the bible heard God (visions, dreams, audible voice, prophecy, etc.). Which, if any of these, have you experienced?

- In what way or ways would you still like to experience God speaking? Have you considered asking Him to speak to you in that way?

5. The author maintains that the more we discover Jesus, the more we discover ourselves. As you pursue Jesus more and more deeply, what is it about yourself you could find?

   - How do you think He really feels about you?

   - What do you think Jesus would say to you about your destiny?

   - How does that make you feel?

   - If you were in His place right now, what would you say to someone else in your group in answer to these questions?

CHAPTER 4

1. The river in Ezekiel 47 is a picture of the Holy Spirit bringing transformation. In what ways have you seen the Spirit bring transformation?

2. Have someone in your group read aloud Ezekiel 47:1-12. What do you think is significant about the fact that the river gets larger and more powerful the farther it moves away from the temple?

3. Discuss what happens to the water of the Sea [Dead Sea] and to the trees because of the water. How does this reflect the work of the Holy Spirit?

4. Keeping in mind Ephesians 3:20, take some time to talk about what it would look like if the Holy Spirit

transformed your city, and jot down some notes. (Have fun with this and take the limits off your imaginations!) Then discuss the question: What would it take for that to happen?

5. Do you know a person or a situation that is in desperate need of the Spirit's transforming work? If appropriate, consider having the group take on this person or situation as a prayer project.

CHAPTER 5

1. This chapter discussed a variety of spiritual phenomena. Which of these, if any, have you seen or experienced?

2. Discuss with the group what the feelings of the members are toward these various phenomena.

3. Have any members of the group seen or experienced phenomena they felt were from the Holy Spirit which were not mentioned in this chapter? List them and talk about them.

   • What are some concerns about these spiritual phenomena?

4. If the Holy Spirit were to bring revival to your church or city, accompanied by unusual phenomena, such as the ones mentioned in this chapter, how would you feel?

   - How much "messiness" would you feel comfortable with, providing you truly believed the Holy Spirit was at work?

5. What are some ways these phenomena should be evaluated, to determine whether or not they are valid works of God?

CHAPTER 6

1. This chapter talks about the importance of evaluating prophetic messages or personal "words" supposedly from God. Have you ever heard a "word" that you knew was not from God? If you feel free to, discuss it with your group. If not, just go on to question 2.

2. Have you ever received a true prophecy or message from God? What effect did it have on you?

3. The rudder of the Church was also discussed in this chapter. Are you connected with a mature Christian or group of mature believers who can help you determine whether you are hearing from God? If so, how have you seen the value of these relationships?

   - How have you experienced the value of knowing Christians outside of your church or different from your background? Can you give some examples?

4. On a scale from 1-10, with 1 being "pathetic" to 10 being "an expert," how would you rate your knowledge of the bible?

   • What are you doing to improve your score?

   • Is there someone who could help you in this process? How could they help?

5. Has God ever spoken to you in a personal way from the bible? Or has the Holy Spirit especially illuminated a passage to you in a fresh way? If appropriate, consider sharing it with the group.

CHAPTER 7

1. In this chapter the author discusses the three main passages of scripture dealing with spiritual gifts. Take some time and discuss the distinctions of these three passages in your group, jotting down your notes.

2. Can you think of any other gifts of the Spirit which may fit the context of First Corinthians 12:8-10? (If you do, please let me know!)

3. Have you personally experienced any of the gifts discussed in this chapter?

   • If so, what are your most memorable experiences of the Spirit's gifts?

4. Are there any of these gifts that you seem to have a particular desire for?

5. Have you ever experienced a physical or emotional healing by the power of the Holy Spirit? Do you feel comfortable discussing it with the group?

6. Have you ever seen or experienced one of these gifts outside of a church setting? What happened?

7. What do you think you or your group could do to experience more of these gifts?

CHAPTER 8

1. Is there someone you know personally (not related to this group) who you can point to as a true example of the love of Jesus? If this is awkward or difficult, think about someone in the bible who best emulated the love of Jesus.

   • What is it about the way they live (or lived) and act (or acted) that reflects the love of Christ?

2. Can you think of a favorite passage of scripture where someone (other than Jesus) demonstrated God's love?

3. Take some time alone and read First Corinthians 13:4-7, inserting your name in the place of each word that describes love, writing those phrases in the space below (for example, "Dan is kind, Dan is

patient…"). Then come back together as a group and talk about how that made you feel.

4. What do you think should be the relationship between the gifts of the Spirit and love?

   • Can you give an example?

5. How would your life change if you learned to love more like Jesus?

CHAPTER 9

1. In Luke 8, Jesus taught about four types of soils, which correspond to four different types of heart condition. Of these, only the last type represents the good heart. Which of the other three types do you see most of the time among the unchurched people you know?

2. God took over twenty years to prepare Joseph's heart before He could fulfill His plans for him. He also took many years to prepare David, after he was anointed by Samuel, before he would become king. Why do you think this process takes so long?

   • What kinds of things is God changing in us to prepare us for greater things?

3. In First Samuel 16:7, we are told that man looks at the outward appearance, but God looks at the heart. What kinds of things does our culture look at in evaluating people?

- Do you think most Christians have values that are very different from those of our culture? Can you support your answer?

4. Can you think of a time when someone was promoted instead of you, or got some form of recognition or attention you felt you deserved? How successfully have you dealt with that issue in your own heart? (Hint: How much peace do you have when the person's name is mentioned?)

5. David was one of the most godly men in the bible. Yet in Psalm 139:23-24, he prayed that God would search his heart to see if there was any wicked way in him. Why is this a good practice, even for the most godly among us?

CHAPTER 10

1. This chapter discusses the importance of wisdom as part of the rudder.

    a. Can you think of a situation in the past few weeks or months where wisdom was needed? (If not, go to part B.) Did the needed wisdom seem to come through from God? If so, how?

    b. How about today? Is there a situation you or a loved one is facing which calls for wisdom?

2. Why do you think it is that wisdom doesn't always come with age?

3. When the Holy Spirit comes in power, many remarkable things happen, including the widespread manifestation of spiritual gifts. So why do you suppose that, even in those Spirit-saturated

environments, leaders don't automatically have wisdom for every situation?

4. This chapter showed how Paul, John Wesley, and others built effective structures, such as discipleship groups and new church plants, to help preserve the harvest. The following is a two-part question:

   a. Do you and your church believe that another "Great Awakening" is on the horizon?

   b. If so, what are you doing to prepare?

5. Dan mentions four ways to obtain wisdom: Through experience, by asking (persistently) for it, through reading God's word, the bible, and by pursuing Jesus with passion. Which of these four paths to wisdom seems the most familiar or appealing to you?

   • Now, which of the other paths to wisdom seems to intrigue you?

CHAPTER 11

1. The author says, "Reaching lost people has always been the top priority of Jesus and the Spirit." On a "priority scale," with 1 being the bottom and 10 being the top priority, where do you think reaching lost people fits on your scale? What does this suggest to you?

2. Was there a particular person who was instrumental in you becoming a believer in Jesus? Do you remember the details of how it all happened? Write the short version below, and if time permits, share your testimony with the group.

3. In Luke 15, Jesus told three parables symbolizing individuals who are "lost." Read the parable of the lost son (sometimes called the "prodigal") and discuss what this story reveals about the heart of the Father toward His lost children.

- Do you know someone like the prodigal? Consider sharing briefly about them with the group (being careful to guard their anonymity).

- What do you think would happen if you were to pray daily that they would find Jesus?

4. In this chapter, the statement was made that there are two things that will atrophy unless we are intentional about going after them: evangelism and the gifts of the Spirit. And the reason is that they both move us out of our comfort zone and they both involve risk.

  - Talk about the feelings that the idea of "evangelism" evokes in you.

CHAPTER 12

1. This chapter refers to the days after Pentecost in Acts 2 and following as "The Pinnacle" of church life as described in the New Testament. List the three things that God did to make this phenomenon happen.

   • Now list the three things that the people did.

2. The author believes that God desires to bring a great revival, and makes seven statements that support his case. Discuss those statements and see if your group comes to the same conclusion. Can you think of some other reasons that lead you to believe another Great Awakening is unfolding?

   • Can you think of some reasons that a great revival may not be coming?

3. One of the things the people did prior to Pentecost is pray. Find out if anyone in your group has

started doing this with a small group yet. Is there any interest?

4. Another thing the people did both before and after Pentecost was to prepare. What kinds of preparation would you and your church need to undertake to get ready for a great revival in your area?

5. The third thing the people did was to proclaim the good news about Jesus and the Kingdom of God.

   • Do you know anyone who regularly does this?

   • Do you have a desire to do more of this?

   • Is there a committed group of people in your church who pray regularly for those who are doing this on a regular basis?

CHAPTER 13

1. Do you feel it's time for the Church in this country to find a "new normal"?

   • Why?

2. How do you feel about the idea of finding a "new normal" for yourself? Are you ready for a more radical discipleship? Why or why not?

3. Read Hosea 10:12. The author shared how God spoke to him from his garden about an unused area in his life. Ask the Holy Spirit to reveal to you an area in your life that needs to be renovated and cultivated in order for you to bear fruit in a new part of your life. Can you discuss this with your group?

4. The author discussed four challenges to breaking out of our old normal: Homeostasis, Distraction, Dissipation, and Indulgence. Which of these presents the greatest challenge to you, and why?

5. This chapter also talks about two actions you could take to break the hold of your old normal and move into the adventure of a new normal: Pursuit and Acceleration. Read and discuss these brief paragraphs.

   - Do either of these stir you? Talk about some ways you could engage in a deeper pursuit or acceleration in order to move forward in your relationship with the Lord.

6. There are six rewards discussed under "The Payoff." Talk about these and see which of these excites you the most.

7. Are you ready for a new adventure in your spiritual life? Are you ready for a new and radical form of Christian discipleship? Consider joining together and embarking on this adventure together. Write down your thoughts below.

About Dan Smith

Dan Smith has been a pastor for 36 years. He currently serves as the Senior Pastor of Vineyard Community Church in Camarillo, California, and oversees fourteen churches in the greater Los Angeles area.

He is available for speaking engagements, and can be reached through his email address, dansmith2@verizon.net, or through his website, www.windandrudder.com. He can also be contacted by phone at (805) 795-7587.